TRANSFORMING TEXTS

Shaun O'Toole

 Routledge
Taylor & Francis Group

LONDON AND NEW YORK

First published 2003 by Routledge
11 New Fetter Lane, London EC4P 4EE

Simultaneously published in the USA and Canada
by Routledge
29 West 35th Street, New York, NY 10001

Routledge is an imprint of the Taylor & Francis Group

Typeset in Galliard by Keystroke, Jacaranda Lodge, Wolverhampton
Printed and bound in Great Britain by TJ International Ltd, Padstow, Cornwall

British Library Cataloguing in Publication Data
A catalogue record for this book is available from the British Library

Library of Congress Cataloging in Publication Data
A catalog record for this book has been requested

ISBN 0–415–28630–1 (hbk)
ISBN 0–415–28631–X (pbk)

For my parents Brian and Jill, and Jane Hale.

CONTENTS

ILLUSTRATIONS

FIGURES

TABLES

PREFACE

ASSESSMENT OBJECTIVES

The AS/A2 specifications in English are governed by assessment objectives (AOs) which break down each of the subjects into component parts and skills. These assessment objectives have been used to create the different modules which together form a sort of jigsaw puzzle. Different objectives are highlighted in different modules, but at the end of AS and again at the end of A2 each of the objectives has been given a roughly equal weighting.

Particular assessment objectives that are focused on in this book are:

English Language and Literature

AO2: in responding to literary and non-literary texts, you must distinguish, describe and interpret variation in meaning and form

AO3: you must respond to and analyse texts, using literary and linguistic concepts and approaches

AO4: you must show understanding of the ways contextual variation and choices of form, style and vocabulary shape the meanings of texts

AO6: you must show expertise and accuracy when writing for a variety of specific purposes and audiences, and you must explain and comment on the choices you have made

---

English Language

AO2: you must show expertise and accuracy when writing for a variety of specific purposes and audiences, and you must explain and comment on the choices you have made

AO3: you must show a systematic approach to analysing texts

AO5: you must analyse the ways contextual factors affect the way texts are written, read and understood

This book aims to help you to:

- Develop your ability to write texts, making them appropriate for their audience and purpose
- Use source materials by editing, rewriting and transforming them for use in your own writing
- Understand better the nature of language variation according to context and over time by using text-transformation as a learning aid
- Write commentaries on the language choices you have made when transforming texts

Each chapter contains a number of exercises. When the exercise introduces a new idea, there will usually be suggestions for answer immediately following. When the exercise checks to see if a point has been understood, suggestions for answer can be found at the back of the book.

ACKNOWLEDGEMENTS

Thanks to: Jane Hale for reading and commenting on drafts; Adrian Beard for good advice and guidance; Angela Goddard for the invitation; Caroline Dickinson for her tape; the staff and students of Itchen College for helping to try out and develop ideas.

'A strange spell in the weather' and 'A quick an easy method to create your own surrealism': extracts from an article by Andrew Graham-Dixon first published in the *Independent*, 26 May 1992.

'Huon Pine' information leaflet, Forestry Commission, Tasmania.

Eyewitness account of Peter Bennett, Imperial War Museum Sound Archive 6087/5/1, 1982.

Extract from Gilda O'Neill, *My East End* © Gilda O'Neill 1999 (Penguin).

Extract from *Lay My Burden Down*, ed. B.A. Botkin (University of Georgia Press, 1945).

Extract from *Shakespeare Made Easy: Macbeth* by Alan Durband (reprinted by permission of Nelson Thornes, 1984).

Extract from Nick Hornby, *Fever Pitch – The Screenplay* © Nick Hornby and Channel 4 International Ltd 1997 (Indigo).

Extract from Nick Hornby, *Fever Pitch* © Nick Hornby 1993 (Indigo).

Extract from *Sense and Sensibility – The Screenplay*, published by Bloomsbury, reprinted by permission of PFD on behalf of Emma Thompson © 1995 by Columbia Pictures, Industries, Inc.

'Killer Yachts' © Martin Corrick, published in the *Guardian*, 27 July 1985.

LANGUAGE THE SOCIAL CHAMELEON

CHAPTER 1

INTRODUCTION

The nature of language is that it is endlessly varying and changing. Language is a kind of chameleon. Like the lizard, it changes its colour and hue to suit the background where it finds itself. The workings of language could also be described by another metaphor from computer imaging. Language is always morphing and changing its form, re-inventing itself. Language is always transforming itself.

This book is about the transformations of language. In this first chapter we shall explore why language varies and changes and how we transform it.

WHAT'S IN A NAME?

Language transforms itself to fit the variety of situations in which it is used. A simple example that illustrates this is our own name. It seems a simple question when someone asks us what our name is. It's Shaun O'Toole. Or is it Shaun? Or Mr O'Toole? Perhaps this question is more complicated than it first seemed.

Exercise 1

Write down the different ways you are named. Note down who calls you this name and in what situation this name is used.

What are the reasons why the form of your name keeps changing?

You could set out your answers as in Table 1.1.

Table 1.1 'Version of your name'

Version of your name	Who uses this version	The situation when this version is used

Suggestions for Answer

The version of our name varies depending on whom we are talking or writing to. To someone I know intimately I might just sign a birthday card from S. When introducing myself to a new class of students I would introduce myself as Shaun O'Toole. Language changes to suit its audience.

The relationship between readers and writers or speakers and listeners can affect the way a name is used. It is currently common practice in business to adopt a friendly and informal address to customers, greeting them by their forename. On other occasions we will be addressed more formally as when a police officer confirms my identity: 'Are you Mr Shaun O'Toole?' Our name might vary depending on the relative status of the people involved in a conversation. When we are at school we are often encouraged to call a male teacher Sir, reinforcing the sense of teachers' authority over their pupils.

What is being discussed may affect the language we use. A doctor may choose my first name to tell me something serious while my boss might call me Mr O'Toole when she wants to reprimand me. The subject matter will affect the language choices we make.

Our purpose in communicating may affect the way we use words. My partner might add an elongated **suffix** onto my name when she wants to ask a favour: 'Shaunie . . . '.

There are some occasions when our name varies because of the medium in which we are using language. It is rare that I speak the form S. O'Toole but I do often write this form. The conventions of e-language (and its intolerance of some forms of punctuation such as the apostrophe) mean that I have generated new versions of my name in e-mails: Shaun.OToole or sotoole. What we are seeing here is the way the **mode** of language used, whether it is spoken, written or electronic, affects the choices we make.

So far we have considered the way aspects of the immediate context can affect the language we use. Our language use is also affected by wider contexts as well. Our names reflect the period in which we were born. Every year newspapers publish lists of the most popular names of the year. Names come and go as fashion changes. This is an example of how language changes over time.

It is also true that other factors affect our names. Gender is a most obvious factor but there are some names that morph depending on whether they apply to a male or a female (e.g. Leslie or Lesley). Research has shown that English names have different structures because of gender: female names are likely to have more **syllables** than male names and are also more likely to end in a spoken vowel sound.

Names vary according to class and ethnicity too. We are all familiar with the Sharon and Tracy jokes picked up in the TV series *Birds of a Feather*. In *Keeping Up Appearances* the character Hyacinth Bucket insisted on transforming the pronunciation of her name to Bouquet in an attempt to escape a working-class background by suggesting greater class and status. My name reflects my Irish family history.

The spelling of my name also reflects a wider cultural and social background. Shaun O'Toole is an Anglicised spelling of the Gaelic version Seán Ó Tuathail. My name bears the marks of the Anglicisation of Irish names in the nineteenth century. This was carried out by the English rulers of Ireland who exerted their cultural control through such linguistic transformations. Brian Friel's play *Translations* explores the significance of this process.

SUMMARY

So far we have explored the immediate factors that shape language variation:

- The nature of the audience
- The relationship between the writer/speaker and their audience
- Subject matter
- Purpose
- The mode of communication

We have also considered the effect of wider social, cultural and historical contexts:

- Period
- Gender
- Class
- Ethnicity
- Politics
- Technology

WHY TRANSFORMING TEXTS IS VALUABLE

Language is always transforming itself – whenever speakers or writers use language they vary their language to suit the context. The language they use bears the stamp of the context for which it was intended. Transforming texts is a useful learning device in exploring how language and context are connected. By doing this we can see much more clearly the distinctive features that texts have and the effects of particular aspects of context.

As speakers and writers, we have to develop a repertoire of styles to suit the different people we deal with, the subjects we have to discuss and the purposes we need to achieve. We need to be able to transform our style and write and speak in a variety of different ways.

When we are writing we often carry out research and go to other sources to provide us with information for use. When we need to use other texts as sources we need to transform them for their new uses.

As you use this book you will employ a number of approaches to transforming texts. You will:

- Make analytical and evaluative comparisons of transformed texts (e.g. comparing a Shakespeare text with its 'Shakespeare Made Easy' version) to explore the nature and effects of transformation
- Do some writing exercises based on texts for transformation (e.g. producing a TV script of a nineteenth-century novel)
- Carry out some focused activities to address particular types of transformation (e.g. point of view, changing a text from spoken to written)

As the book progresses we shall use some explicit, technical descriptions of language to explain what is happening in texts and exercises. The first time a technical term is used it will be **emboldened**. An explanation can be found in the Glossary at the back of the book.

TRANSFORMING TEXTS

The French writer Raymond Queneau wrote a book called *Exercises de Style* (translated as *Exercises in Style* by Barbara Wright). In this book Queneau tells the story of a man he sees on a bus. The man complains to another passenger who has jostled him. Later the same day Queneau sees the man again. He is being advised by a friend to get another button sewn onto his coat. This may not strike you as much of a story to write a book about. You may be even more concerned to find out that Queneau goes on to tell this same story ninety-nine times!

Queneau retells the same story to explore the ways language varies and changes. Each time he tells the story he tells it in a different way. In the English translation one version of the story is told in a West Indian dialect. In another version the story is told in the form of an official letter. In yet another version the story is told using only passive verbs. The books shows us the shape-shifting nature of language and all the permutations and combinations it can make when being used.

In 1992 the *Independent* published a review of an exhibition of the paintings of René Magritte. Magritte was a Belgian surrealist artist. In his paintings he tried to disrupt our normal ways of seeing things, and makes us see things anew by producing unusual and unexpected combinations of images.

The review was entitled 'Ceci n'est pas une critique' (meaning 'This is not a review') with the strapline 'Rene Magritte played with perceptions while painting in style(s). Andrew Graham-Dixon responds in kind.' It would seem the reviewer had been inspired by Raymond Queneau. Instead of writing a normal art review he wrote a series of short texts about Magritte's painting, each in a different style, inspired by the paintings in the exhibition. He wrote in the style of a user's guide, a recipe, a weather forecast, a travel book, a phrase book, a book of philosophy and a psychoanalytical text. His point was to make the reader see the paintings from a new perspective. He kept transforming the style of the review into the style of another text.

Now it is time for you to do some limbering up ready to begin Transforming Texts. You are going to do two exercises. One is analytical to make you think about the features of different styles. The second exercise is creative to start you writing and transforming your styles of language use.

Exercise 2

Below you will see two extracts from Andrew Graham Dixon's review. One is written in the style of a weather forecast and the other is written as a recipe. What aspects of language reflect the different styles he is using to write about the paintings?

Text A

A strange spell in the weather

From the archives of the Belgian Meteorological Office:

Forecast: The weather will continue unsettling. Large banks of cumulus are expected to remain motionless over western regions of the country while there will be sudden showers of dead birds in isolated areas. Large conurbations will experience mainly blue skies, giving way later in the day to sudden storms. Heavy precipitation of businessmen expected in Brussels and Ghent. **Outlook:** A warm week, with long periods of intense and curiously troubling sunshine.

Sudden showers: *Golconde (detail)*

Figure 1.1 'A strange spell in the weather'

Extract from an article by Andrew Graham-Dixon first published in the *Independent*, 26 May 1992

Text B

A quick and easy method to create your own Surrealism

Plat du jour: *Le Portrait* (detail)

From *René and Georgette's Belgian Cookery Course* (**Pan Books, 1967**):

TOILE SURREALE

Ingredients

1 medium sized canvas (you can buy these ready primed from most good art suppliers)
4 tablespoons drab domestic interior
4 oz assorted symbolic elements
2 fl oz northern light (you will find most Italian brands are simply too warm)
3 or 4 good-sized businessmen (ask the butcher to leave the heads on)
Finely chopped sentences for decoration

Method

First mix the light and interior well, until you have a smooth mixture, without any distracting lumps. Then apply to the canvas using swift dabbing brushstrokes to lay down an even background before applying your substantial motifs. This can be tricky for beginners but once you get the hang of it you'll find it second nature and your friends will be most impressed that you don't buy your Surrealism ready-made! You shouldn't be aiming for flourishes of paint or conspicuous technical skill by the way; as René says, 'I always try to make sure that the actual painting isn't noticed, that it is as little visible as possible.'

Put aside and allow to set at room temperature before adding your symbolic motifs and businessmen. There's no hard and fast rule here but it's best if you get a nice contrast in textures and taste. You can do a lot worse than follow Lautréamont's classic principle of 'the chance encounter of an umbrella and a sewing machine on a dissecting table'! Finally dress the resulting canvas with proper nouns, according to taste. A chilled bottle of Belgian Grattime, an instantly appealing wine but with a deceptively long finish, goes very well with this meal. Oh, and one last tip: hand-decorate that wine bottle, preferably with the figure of a naked woman. Enjoy!!!!

Figure 1.2 'A quick and easy method to create your own Surrealism'

Extract from an article by Andrew Graham-Dixon first published in the *Independent*, 26 May 1992

Suggestions for Answer – Text A

Andrew Graham-Dixon has chosen to write in a weather forecast style to explore the unsettling effects of Magritte's painting in which the painter shows the way a town fills up with businessmen.

Semantics

The weather forecast style is suggested by the use of a **semantic field** of weather features, 'storms', 'showers' and so on. There is also some use of technical weather vocabulary such as the cloud type 'cumulus'. As this is a written forecast a high level of formality is employed with words such as 'conurbations' and 'precipitation'. The semantic field of time is also used to indicate when the weather will occur and its duration.

There are also words that do not fit into the semantic fields of a forecast such as dead birds and businessmen. These are present to reflect Magritte's painting with its raining businessmen.

Grammar

Verbs are used to indicate future time, e.g. 'will continue', reflecting the forecast's predictive nature. **Passive** forms of **verbs** occur (e.g. 'are expected') instead of **active** forms such as 'we expect'. This is conventional for formal written weather forecasts. There is evidence of **ellipsis** for economy: **auxiliary verbs** such as 'are' are sometimes omitted. There is the use of **adverbials of place** (e.g. 'over western regions of the country') that signal where the forecast applies. **Proper nouns** are also used to indicate the places affected by the weather forecast: 'Brussels and Ghent'.

Suggestions for Answer – Text B

Inspired by part of a painting depicting a dish on a dining-table, Andrew Graham-Dixon uses the recipe form to discuss the nature of Surrealism as a style of painting.

Semantics

The recipe style is created by the use of a semantic field of measurements: 'medium sized', 'tablespoons'. There is also a field of cooking methods and actions: 'mix', 'put aside and allow to set'. There is also vocabulary from the field of art: 'brush-strokes', 'motifs', 'paint' and so on.

Grammar

The text makes uses of **imperatives** to guide the reader through a series of actions that will create a surrealist painting: 'mix', 'apply'. There is direct address using the second-person **pronoun** 'you' and colloquial parentheses and advice to suggest the voice of the expert cook talking to the reader that is so typical of many recipes: 'Oh, and one last tip'. There are adverbials of time such as 'First' and 'Finally' which reflect the chronological structure of recipe texts.

Exercise 3

Create a sequence of events or a simple story of your own (like Raymond Queneau's). Alternatively choose the bare bones of a story you know (e.g. from a book, a film or even a fairy story). Choose two different styles and rewrite the story in each style. Write a brief commentary on how you used language differently in each version.

(You may like to look at suggestions for answer to Exercise 2 to give you some ideas of how to do this.)

SUMMARY

In this chapter we have explored:

- Why the language of texts varies
- The effect of the immediate and wider contexts on language choices in terms of vocabulary, grammar and presentation
- How we transform our style of writing for specific purposes and audiences
- How we can explain and comment on the way we transform our style in different situations

Transforming texts will be helpful to you in preparing for AS and A Level examinations because you will be able to:

- Understand more fully how and why language varies in different situations
- Write in different styles

CHAPTER 2

TRANSFORMING TEXTS FOR DIFFERENT AUDIENCES AND PURPOSES

INTRODUCTION

In this chapter we will explore how to change the language of texts so that they are suitable for new audiences and purposes: the skills of editorial writing or textual recasting. To begin with we shall think about the key principles that underlie the way texts are put together: selection and combination and Halliday's three functions of language. These principles will help us to see how to transform the language of texts. A case study ends the chapter, exploring how to simplify an informational text for a younger audience.

HOW LANGUAGE VARIES AND CHANGES: SELECTION AND COMBINATION

There are two main principles that govern how language varies and changes: selection and combination. These two principles are very powerful tools for under-standing how language works. Thinking about them will help us understand how to transform texts effectively.

If we consider briefly how children acquire language we can see these two principles at work. When children begin to talk they go through what is known as the one-word stage. At this point in their development they can only say one word at a time – at the very start they may literally be able to say only one word! At this stage language does not vary much at all. Their one word has to do a lot of jobs. If their first word is 'daddy', that word might have to communicate *there's daddy*, *get daddy*, *feed me* and so on. This hypothetical state does not last long. Soon the child develops many more words and starts to select which one is appropriate in each new situation.

The next stage of development is when children move into the two-word stage. They begin to combine two words together to convey more complex ideas with greater precision; for example, *mummy juice* (*mummy get the juice*) *daddy play, play ball*. The child is now making its first use of the combination of words into larger units.

When we are looking at transforming texts we are operating these two fundamental principles of how language works: selection and combination.

It is helpful to consider a text as a number of slots that can be filled with different selections and which can be put together in a number of different ways. If we confine ourselves to a simple sentence to begin with we can see how these ideas work. Consider this sentence:

The person walked down the street.

It is made up of six slots that have been combined to make up this sentence. We could take any slot and begin to transform the sentence by making different selections that could fill the slot:

The	person	walked	down	the	street.
The	woman	walked	down	the	street.
The	aunt	walked	down	the	street.
The	pensioner	walked	down	the	street.
The	OAP	walked	down	the	street.
The	senior citizen	walked	down	the	street.

The changes we make here subtly transform the meaning and focus of this sentence. By changing the word within one slot we are drawing on the lexical resources of the language. We can use **synonyms** with slightly different **denotations** and **connotations** that would shape the way we see the person described. We could also draw on different levels of formality or use technical or non-technical language. If we started to make changes to the other slots, the number of potential transformations is huge.

As well as the selections in each slot we could create variations by combining the slots in different ways:

Down the street walked the woman.
Down the street the woman walked.

We could also transform the sentence further by adding further slots to create new combinations:

The old woman walked down the street.
The old woman in a grey coat walked down the street.
The old woman in a grey coat walked slowly down the street.

The old woman in a grey coat walked slowly down the street after lunch.
The old woman in a grey coat walked slowly down the street after lunch and left her familiar world behind.

From here we could go on to add more sentences and think about the ways in which they could be laid out and organised into a whole text. The number of possible transformations is endless. As you can see, it is the power to select and combine that enables us to create a huge variety of different texts. When we transform a text we need to think about what slots we require and how we are going to fill them.

THE FUNCTIONS OF LANGUAGE

The linguist M.A.K. Halliday has suggested that the language in a text has three broad functions:

- The ideational function – to represent ideas and information
- The interpersonal function – to create and maintain social relationships
- The textual function – to organise and structure texts

When we are transforming a text for a new audience and purpose we need to pay attention to these three functions and consider how to use language in different ways to fulfil these functions. We must ask:

- How do we need to transform the way the text presents ideas?
- How do we need to transform the way the text engages with its audience?
- How do we need to transform the way the text organises itself?

As we transform a text we will achieve the transformation by selecting different vocabulary items and combining words in different ways.

Let us consider a specific example. You are writing a text for a pressure group that is opposed to genetically modified (GM) foods. The text is a letter to shoppers at a supermarket. Its purpose is to persuade shoppers to lobby their supermarket to ban GM foods in their stores. You have been provided with a series of scientific briefing papers about GM foods to provide you with the facts for your letter.

In this situation you may need to transform the language in your sources to fulfil your new text's ideational functions. You will probably need to express complex scientific ideas in a simple way. You may want to persuade your reader to see GM foods in a particular way. Perhaps you might call them 'Frankenfoods' with its connotations of horror and tampering disastrously with nature. 'Genetically modified foods' sounds much more scientific and controlled, a more acceptable image perhaps. The way you select your words and put your text together will be determined by your ideational purposes and the way you want to represent things.

The interpersonal dimension will also affect the way you put your text together. You will need to consider your audience and how to address them. The scientific briefing papers are likely to be impersonal and formal in style. It might be better for you to use a more familiar and direct address to your audience. Addressing them using the pronoun 'we' would be a good strategy to create some fellow feeling and get them on your side. Using 'you' will direct the issues at them personally. You might want to use questions and commands. You might want to transform the declarative mood of your informational source texts to challenge your reader and lead them into action.

You will also need to transform the way your source texts fulfil the textual purposes of language. As briefing papers they may be only a series of bullet points. On a very simple level you might want to adopt a letter layout. You might want to use a font that suggests handwriting to make your appeal seem more personal. You might want to use subheadings between paragraphs to foreground the key points in your argument.

REWRITING FOR A NEW AUDIENCE AND PURPOSE

The following text was used as part of the source material in a task to write an extract for an educational reference book entitled *Unusual Trees of the World*. The reference book was to be aimed at young children. The source was taken from a Tasmanian Forestry Commission leaflet and was aimed at an adult audience. Here is the beginning of the source leaflet.

The tree

Huon pine (*Lagarostrobos franklinii*, formerly *Dacrydium franklinii*) is the only member of the genus of *Lagarostrobos* in Tasmania, and it is related to species in Chile, Malaysia and New Zealand. It is endemic to Tasmania, ie it grows naturally in Tasmania and nowhere else.

Huon pine is easily recognised by its feathery foliage and hanging branches; it is similar in appearance to the common cypress.

Huon pine produces pollen and seeds in small, inconspicuous cones with male and female cones on separate trees.

Selecting the Right Words: Transforming the Vocabulary

Let us begin by considering this passage from the point of view of its selection of vocabulary. There are a number of words and types of vocabulary that would be difficult for younger readers.

The text adopts a formal and scientific style. As a result it uses Latin names for the tree. It also uses a range of technical biological terms such as 'genus', 'species' and 'endemic'. It is interesting that the text presupposes that the word 'endemic' may not be familiar to the reader as it glosses its meaning: 'ie it grows naturally in Tasmania and nowhere else.' The text also assumes that the reader knows what pollen is.

Its vocabulary sometimes draws on words of French or Latin origin. Such words are often part of the higher formality registers of the English language. It is words that are of Anglo-Saxon and Viking origin that make up our more everyday and **colloquial** register. The word 'foliage' is of French origin and is linked to the French word *feuille*. The word 'produce' came into English from a Latin verb *producere* meaning to bring or lead forward. The words 'similar' and 'appearance' came into English from French and can be traced back further to a Latin root. 'Inconspicuous' is a word of Latin origin.

If we were to transform this text for a younger audience it would seem necessary to alter the selection of vocabulary by removing the Latinate terms and finding **synonyms** for the scientific and high register terms. Here is a rewritten version of the text:

The tree

Huon pine is the only member of its family of pine trees in Tasmania, and it is related to kinds of pines in Chile, Malaysia and New Zealand. It grows naturally in Tasmania and nowhere else.

Huon pine is easily recognised by its feathery leaves and hanging branches; it looks like the common cypress.

Huon pine makes pollen and seeds in small, not easily seen cones with male and female cones on separate trees.

Changing the Combinations: Transforming the Grammar

As well as considering the selection of vocabulary, we should also look at the ways in which this text combines its words. The first sentence is a **compound sentence** with two **clauses**. The second sentence is a **complex sentence** with two clauses. Another two-clause compound sentence follows this. The final paragraph contains a **simple sentence**.

If we return to the original text we could simplify the patterns of grammar for our audience by using more simple sentences:

The tree

Huon pine (*Lagarostrobos franklinii*, formerly *Dacrydium franklinii*) is the only member of the genus of *Lagarostrobos* in Tasmania. It is related to species in Chile, Malaysia and New Zealand. It is endemic to Tasmania. It grows naturally in Tasmania and nowhere else.

Huon pine is easily recognised by its feathery foliage and hanging branches. It is similar in appearance to the common cypress.

Huon pine produces pollen and seeds in small, inconspicuous cones with male and female cones on separate trees.

This transformation still leaves two grammatical features that we might want to alter. In the second paragraph there is a passive verb structure:

Huon pine is easily recognised by its feathery foliage and hanging branches.

These passive structures are more difficult to decode. The usual active structure puts the agent (the person or thing doing the action) before the verb. In the passive this is altered. The affected (the person or thing on the receiving end of the action) comes first before the verb. The agent can be left out completely. Apart from its complexity, the passive is a feature typical of formal and especially scientific styles. It is also used because it creates a more impersonal style by allowing the agent not to be mentioned. We could transform the passive into the active:

You can easily recognise Huon pine by its feathery foliage and hanging branches.

There is another passive in this sentence:

It is related to species in Chile, Malaysia and New Zealand.

We could change this to:

Related species grow in Chile, Malaysia and New Zealand.

A second grammatical feature we might alter is the use of the **prepositional phrase** 'with male and female cones on separate trees' in the final sentence. This adds an extra idea into a simple, but long sentence. We could turn it into a separate sentence:

Huon pine produces pollen and seeds in small, inconspicuous cones. Male and female cones are on separate trees.

Having considered issues of both selection and combination we can now complete a transformation of this piece of text:

The tree

Huon pine is the only member of its family of pine trees in Tasmania. There are other pines like it in Chile, Malaysia and New Zealand. It grows naturally in Tasmania and nowhere else.

You can easily recognise Huon pine by its feathery leaves and hanging branches. It looks like the common cypress.

Huon pine makes pollen and seeds in small, not easily seen cones. Male and female cones are on separate trees.

Avoiding Assumptions: What We Expect the Reader to Know

Apart from the relative complexity of the grammar and vocabulary of this text there is another issue we should consider regarding how easy a child would find it to understand. There are a number of words that rely on the child's general knowledge for understanding.

The text makes presuppositions about the reader's geographical and botanical knowledge. It is assumed that the reader knows where Tasmania, Chile, Malaysia and New Zealand are. It is also assumed that the reader will know what a common cypress is. The text relies on the reader making the connection that a cypress is in fact another type of tree.

To deal with these matters a transformation of this text would need to do something rather more radical than changing word choice or grammatical structure. Perhaps we could highlight or asterisk words and add a word box (a useful synonym for glossary) at the bottom of the page to explain some of the words, such as 'pollen'. This has the advantage of not cluttering up the main text with too much explanation of terms.

On the other hand such a device demands that the reader knows how to cross-refer in a text. It requires sophisticated knowledge of how educational genres of texts work. There may also be a case for using an illustration. A map of the world would help locate the spread of these trees.

In the transformations that we have made to this text we have stripped away all the biological and botanical vocabulary to make the text accessible to its reader. However, it is important that we think about the text's purposes. It is meant to be educational. As well as being accessible to young readers it should perhaps also introduce them to some technical concepts such as genus and species.

This is where the provision of a word box or another textual strategy might allow the term to be used, explained and understood. It is a common feature of some educational texts that they use very simple grammatical structures for accessibility. The vocabulary and ideas are none the less quite sophisticated. They are introduced and explained in simple steps, however. The simplicity of the sentence structure enables the reader to concentrate on the ideas.

Exercise 1

Below you will find another section of the source text about the Huon pine. Transform the text so that it is suitable for a young reader in the new text *Unusual Trees of the World*. Comment on the changes you have made to the language of the text.

Suggestions for answer to this exercise may be found at the back of the book on page 79.

History

The timber has been highly prized since the early days of the colony. One of the reasons for establishing a convict settlement on Sarah Island, Macquarie Harbour in 1821 was for harvesting Huon pine from the Gordon River.

For decades 'piners' worked the west coast rivers under gruelling conditions, seeking out the trees which grew not only on the alluvial river banks but often up the nearby slopes.

After the trees were felled they were manhandled to the river edges to take advantage of the fact that the Huon pine is one of the few native timbers which floats when green. As flood waters bore the logs downstream men worked from their specially built punts to free them and keep them moving on their way to a log boom built across the river and then onto the mills.

SUMMARY

In this chapter we have:

- Explored the way texts are put together according to the principles of selection and combination
- Considered how transforming texts involves manipulating the ideational, interpersonal and textual functions of language
- Transformed a text to suit a new audience and purpose by paying close attention to the selection of vocabulary, grammatical combinations, address and presentation

This work should help you:

- Transform and rewrite sources in editorial or recasting examination and coursework tasks

CHANGING MODES: TRANSFORMING SPEECH AND WRITING

CHAPTER 3

INTRODUCTION

In this chapter we shall look at transforming speech into writing and written language into a spoken style. We shall begin by looking at transcriptions of speech and how they can be converted into written texts. This will reveal the differences between spoken and written language and prepare you for transforming spoken accounts in analytical and editorial tasks. Finally we shall look at how to create a spoken voice when you are asked to adopt a first-person style when carrying out rewriting tasks.

TRANSCRIBING SPOKEN LANGUAGE: TRANSFORMING SPEECH INTO WRITING

One of the most common ways linguists transform spoken language is when they transcribe it. In order to study the nature of speech we need to be able to freeze it so that we can see more easily what is going on. People other than linguists also transcribe language. Spoken language is transcribed in court to keep records of what is said. Journalists also transcribe what people have said in interviews. When they are preparing a book, writers and oral historians produce written versions of what interviewees say.

Text A: Gas Masks is a transcription of a person's spoken account of his memories of using gas masks during the Second World War. It was made from a taped collection called *The Home Front 1939–1945* to be used as part of an A Level examination question. Before it could be used the examination board had to ask for copyright permission from the publishers, the Imperial War Museum. They were very happy to give permission but suggested that they had a better and clearer transcription that could be used. Where the examiners wanted to show all the pauses and hesitations, the Imperial War Museum had edited out these **non-fluency features** and had clarified **sentence** boundaries. The version below contains all the original non-fluency features.

The next text, *Text B: Bombing,* was used in another examination paper. It was taken from Gilda O'Neill's book *My East End.* In this book she reports the memories of people who lived in the East End. This text is about the Blitz in the Second World

War. Gilda O'Neill transcribed the accounts she was given by the East Enders whom she interviewed. Her method of transcription was different from that of the person who transcribed *Text A: Gas Masks*.

Exercise 1

In what ways is the spoken language presented differently in Text A and Text B?

Text A: Gas Masks

Transcription key

(.) = micropause
.h = intake of breath
wh. = incomplete word

well I suppose it was .h erm it it looked (.) something like er a baked bean tin affair on the on the front that had a lot of holes in it and the rest was rubber that went (.) right over covered the whole of your face underneath your chin round towards your ears and over your head .h you couldn't breathe particularly easily er and I think it was like .h er you know when you go to the dentist or had gas at the dentist you you fought against it for a bit .h but once you got used to the idea and that's why of course we had lessons .h erm with them (.) was to erm get used to the idea erm and wh. if you were sensible then they they didn't fog up and you could cope

Eyewitness account of Peter Bennett,
Imperial War Museum Sound Archive 6087/5/1, 1982

Text B: Bombing

We'd heard there'd been a really bad raid in Poplar and I just wanted to get home to see if my family were all right, but they said at work that I had to wait in the shelter till it was over. As soon as the all clear went, I was off. I don't know how I got there, I don't remember, but I know when I did I saw our place had had a direct hit. I nearly died on the spot, but a neighbour came over and said, 'Don't worry. They're all right. They were out. They salvaged some of your stuff and they've gone looking for somewhere to stay. I said I'd tell you.' I was so relieved. It wasn't an unusual sight where we lived, close to the docks, seeing someone with their stuff on a barrow looking for somewhere empty after their place had copped it.

Gilda O'Neill, *My East End* (Penguin)

Suggestions for Answer

Text A: Gas Masks is a transcription that is designed to reveal some of the features of spoken language. It does not use the conventions of written language such as punctuation to mark sentence divisions. (Sentences are really only a feature of writing. We use clauses in speech but do not shape them into sentences in the way we do in writing.)

Text B: Bombing is also a transcription but one which tidies up the spoken language and makes it easier to read and follow in written form. Because we often use speech in face-to-face situations it employs methods of communicating that are necessary and clear in this context. They are not always so clear when transcribed exactly and we have to try to reconstruct how things were said.

Here are some of the features of spoken language that occur in *Text A: Gas Masks*:

- **Fillers**
- **False starts**
- **Pauses**
- Intakes of breath
- Repetition
- Incomplete **grammatical blends** and structures
- No sentence boundaries

These features occur because speech is often spontaneous and there is no opportunity to correct any errors – we cannot redraft speech without repeating it all over again. Pauses and intakes of breath sometimes reflect the breaks in grammatical units of sense, rather like punctuation. Other non-fluency features can be a monitoring effect of the face-to-face situation of much speech. It can be a sign that the speaker is looking for confirmation of understanding and response from the listener.

In *Text B: Bombing* the non-fluency features found in Text A have been edited out. The grammatical structures have also been completed and sentence boundaries are employed to make it easier to follow the sense.

Exercise 2 – Textual Transformation

Rewrite Text A to make it suitable to be published alongside Text B in Gilda O'Neill's book which is an anthology of people's memories and accounts of life in the East End of London.

Comment on how you have managed to retain some of the text's spoken style.

Suggestions for an answer to this exercise may be found at the back of the book on page 80.

TRANSFORMING AN AUDIOTAPE INTO A LETTER

The text below is a transcription made from an audio-cassette sent by a daughter (aged 23) to her mother. The daughter was working in Japan as an English teacher.

Text C: Audiotape Home

Transcription key

(.) micropause	(1.0) pause in seconds
. (e.g. st.) incomplete word	.h intake of breath
:: elongation of sound	

Notes: Sonia is another English teacher; Tomoko teaches Japanese; *Side by Side* is the title of a textbook for teaching English which features a character called Patti Williams.

um (1.0) so what have I been doing (1.0) um we:::ll (2.0) .h yesterday was Monday and I was in the office all day and I discovered that I've got a new Side by Side class ye::s that's exactly what I need so I'm doing nine hours of Side by Side in one week .h um do you know there's still er Sonia's never taught Side by Side and she's been here for over a year and a half but er .h still huh we can't all have the pleasure (1.0) of knowing the text backwards can we I'm I'm back to page um twenty-seven now which is .h I can tell without (.) thinking about it it is where's Patti Williams what's she doing and (.) to be honest Patti Williams is really irritating because she's forever cleaning her bicycle in the parking lot which is like one of those completely meaningless sentences (.) .h anyway erm yeah Sunday was cool probably told you so yeah I must've done you told you I met my ne::w extra-curricular Japanese teacher who's called Tomoko (.) To (.) mo (.) ko (.) which I st. which I don't really like as a Japanese name it's too f. masculine Tom Tomoko but erm (1.0) she's really nice as I say she's 23 she's in the same situation as me (.) .h erm so we sat and I (.) probably told you we sat for two hours and discussed exactly what actions to do to Twinkle Twinkle Little Star (.) it was quite cool (.) and then erm (1.0) yeh I've just been faffing around and I did my usual stuff on a Sunday night I I erm get my cleaning stuff out and I do all my washing up and all my drying up an' stuff like that an' I clean my stove an' do my fridge an' I do my washing an' some ironing an' stuff like that and (2.0) erm actually yesterday I decided to buy a pinny (1.0) which was probably one of the saddest things I've ever bought but they do have some nice ones over here it's kind of catching the erm most Japanese (.) housewifey women wear these kind of overall jobs I think you call it a tabard

Although there are lots of reasons why the daughter chose to produce a tape, we are now going to convert what she said into letter form. This will enable us to view in close detail the differences between spoken and written language. The benefit of this conversion is that it isolates the change of mode. The audience, purpose and content will remain constant. The only difference is the shift of mode. This will clarify the nature of spoken and written language.

Writing is often more planned and can be redrafted so that it tends to contain fewer non-fluency features. Speech realises words as sounds and not as written symbols. This means that words are not always pronounced as they are spelled. There are also non-verbal aspects of speech such as stress, volume, intonation, pace and elongation.

Exercise 3 – Removing Non-fluency and Non-verbal Aspects of Speech

Remove all the evidence of spoken non-fluency and features of the speaker's pronunciation of her words from the transcription.

What sorts of features have you had to remove from the text?

Suggestions for an answer to this exercise may be found at the back of the book on page 81.

Exercise 4 – Inserting Sentence Punctuation

Transform the text further towards a written form by adding in sentence punctuation. To what extent is the sentence structure of your transformed text typical of a written text?

Suggestions for an answer to this exercise may be found at the back of the book on page 82.

Exercise 5 – Transforming Vocabulary and Grammar

Look at the version of the text below. Certain features of the text have been italicised. Would you transform these features or not?

So what have I been doing?[1] *Well*[2] yesterday was Monday and I was in the office all day and I discovered that I've got a new Side by Side class. *Yes that's exactly what I need*[3] so I'm doing nine hours of Side by Side in one week. Do you know Sonia's never taught Side by Side and she's been here for over a year and a half but still we can't all have the pleasure of knowing the text backwards can we? I'm back to page twenty-seven now which I can tell without thinking about it is 'Where's Patti Williams? What's she doing?' and to be honest Patti Williams is really irritating because she's forever cleaning

continued

her bicycle in the parking lot which is *like*[4] one of those completely meaningless sentences.

Anyway[2] *yeah*[5] Sunday was cool. *Probably*[6] *told you so. Yeah*[5] *I must've done.*[6] I met my new extra-curricular Japanese teacher who's called Tomoko, To-mo-ko, which I don't really like as a Japanese name. It's too masculine: Tom Tomoko, but she's really nice *as I say*[7]. She's 23. She's in the same situation as me and I probably told you we sat for two hours and discussed exactly what actions to do to Twinkle Twinkle Little Star. It was quite cool.

I've just been *faffing*[8] around and I did my usual stuff on a Sunday night. I get my cleaning stuff out and I do all my washing up and all my drying up and *stuff like that*[9] and I clean my stove and do my fridge and I do my washing and some ironing and stuff like that and actually yesterday I decided to buy a pinny which was probably one of the saddest things I've ever bought but they do have some nice ones over here. It's kind of catching. Most Japanese *housewifey women*[10] wear these kind of overall *jobs*[9]. I think you call it a tabard.

1. *So what have I been doing?* This question could be transformed into a statement that would act as a topic sentence for a paragraph about work. 'At work I've been assigned a new Side by Side class.' We might want to retain the question because it will make the letter sound more conversational and it simulates some interaction with the mother.
2. *Well/Anyway* These words are typical spoken **discourse markers**. The 'Well' is what may be called a **starter**, meaning 'Hold on, I'm going to say something now'. The 'Anyway' acts to indicate a shift of topic. Are these necessary in a well-organised letter? Probably not, as the reader has time to process the text more slowly and needs less help in having the structure signalled. If we keep them we can still make the text sound as if the daughter is speaking.
3. *Yes that's exactly what I need* The use of tone of voice and present **tense** could be transformed into the past tense: 'which was exactly what I needed'. If we retain it we can give a greater sense of the daughter's attitudes and it is more dramatic.
4. *Like* This is a monitoring feature. It is often used as a hedge in spoken language. Speakers use it to make their points less assertively, seeking agreement or support from their listener. In a non-face-to-face situation we might omit it, particularly when planning what we are saying.
5. *Yeah* This reflects the spontaneous way the daughter is composing the audiotape and having a conversation with herself. We could omit this in a planned letter as she would have time to think about what she wants to say.
6. *Probably told you so/Yeah I must've done* As with the 'Yeah' this could be omitted, as in a letter the time available to think before committing herself to paper would enable her to remember what she has or has not told her mother.

7. *As I say*   This **comment clause** might be omitted in a written version as she has not mentioned the idea previously in the text itself. The verb 'say' is also not strictly precise in a piece of writing although it is customary to use this word.

8. *Faffing*   Speech is often seen as more informal than writing. Perhaps we could replace this with a less colloquial expression: 'I haven't been doing anything very interesting.' This would lose some of the colour of the daughter's expression and reveal less of her attitude. The word 'faffing' is not inappropriate to her relationship with her mother, as it would seem she would say it to her. Why not write it then?

9. *Stuff like that/jobs*   Both of these expressions are typical of the inexplicitness of speech. In writing we might omit them or provide more precise examples or words with more time available to consider what we want to write. We could say 'and other domestic jobs'. This would affect the tone, however, and lose the sense of the daughter's distaste for the domestic routines she feels trapped by. 'Jobs' could be replaced by 'garments' but the shift of formality would jar.

10. *Housewifey women*   Here the daughter shows the creativity of speech as she coins a new adjective. In writing she might have just used 'housewives' or 'women who are housewives' or even characterised the social group further as 'houseproud women who like to look after their home'. In all these cases the written version has the benefit of more time to find the exact word. What is lost is the creativity of the original and the humorous picture she is conveying (as well as her separation of herself from such domestic creatures!). Perhaps we would leave this as it is.

In analysing the features of speech that could be transformed we have often decided to leave them alone. In the first two stages of transformation we made more essential changes as we altered features that were connected to the physical channel of the texts. In this third stage we have been considering linguistic features which sound like speech but which can none the less still appear in writing. It is worth remembering that speech and writing exist on a continuum. The contrasts between the language of the audiotape and a linguistics textbook would be greater. It is also the case that the language of a text is not just an effect of the mode. We could make this tape sound much more written. However, the daughter, even if she did write a letter, would probably still want to make it sound quite chatty. This is because she is writing about informal subjects as a form of social contact with her mother.

SUMMARY

So far we have looked at the distinctive features of speech that would be transformed when turning a text into written format. The following are features you might want to comment on in a spoken text or which you might need to pay attention to when converting speech into writing:

- Non-fluency features (pauses, false starts, blends)
- Non-verbal aspects of speech (e.g. pronunciation, intonation, elongation of sounds)
- Interactive features (questions, monitoring features)
- Discourse markers (e.g. well, so)
- Inexplicit expressions (e.g. like that)
- Use of first **person** and present tense
- Colloquial and informal vocabulary
- Lack of sentence boundaries and punctuation
- Use of 'and' to link clauses.

CREATING A SPOKEN VOICE

Sometimes we need to create a spoken voice when we are writing. You might be writing a dramatic monologue such as one of Alan Bennett's *Talking Heads* as a piece of coursework. You might have some editorial writing or recasting to do where you have been asked to convey information through the use of a dramatised first-person account. How can we create such a style? The first step is to look at an example of a written text that is designed to represent the spoken voice.

Exercise 6 – Analysing How a Spoken Voice is Conveyed

Read the extract on page 27. It is taken from a book about slavery in the USA, *Lay My Burden Down*, edited by B.A. Botkin. It is written to represent the spoken voice of an ex-slave, Jenny Proctor, who recounted her experiences in her nineties.

What linguistic features suggest her spoken voice?

Text D: Jenny Proctor

I's hear tell of them good slave days, but I ain't never seen no good times then. My mother's name was Lisa, and when I was a very small child I hear that driver going from cabin to cabin as early as 3 o'clock in the morning, and when he comes to our cabin he say, 'Lisa, Lisa, git up from there and git that breakfast.' My mother, she was cook, and I don't recollect nothing 'bout my father. If I had any brothers and sisters I didn't know it. We had old ragged huts made out of poles and some of the cracks chinked up with mud and moss and some of them wasn't. We didn't have no good beds, just scaffolds nailed up to the wall out of poles and the old ragged bedding throwed on them. That sure was hard sleeping, but even that feel good to our weary bones after them long hard days' work in the fields. I 'tended to the children when I was a little gal and tried to clean the house just like Old Miss tells me to. Then soon as I was ten years old Old Master, he say, 'Git this here nigger to that cotton patch.'

B.A. Botkin (ed.) *Lay My Burden Down*
(University of Georgia Press, 1945)

Suggestions for Answer – Jenny's Spoken Style

There are several features that suggest Jenny's spoken voice. We can think about these in a number of ways.

1. Features that reflect the channel of speech, i.e. features that reflect the actual sounds of her language.
2. Features that reflect the situation of speaking, e.g. the shared context of speaker and listener who are face to face.
3. Features that reflect the identity of the speaker. Spoken English is more marked by the identity of the speaker than written language. As a consequence accent and dialect features are often seen. So too are **idiolectal** features that reflect the personal style of a speaker.

First-person perspective

Jenny uses first-person pronouns such as 'I' and 'we' which reflect her speaking situation as she tells us about her memories and experiences.

Use of dialogue and direct speech

Jenny uses the words of others in her narrative. These lend authenticity and vitality to the account.

Non-standard verb forms

Jenny uses the form 'has' ('s) in the first-person present tense of the verb 'to have'. In **standard English** the form would be 'have'. She uses a non-standard form when using the **past participle** of the verb 'to hear' in line 1: 'I's hear tell' which would be 'I've heard tell' in standard English. Later when she uses the past tense of the verb 'to hear' she uses a form with no suffix, unlike standard English. The non-standard form 'ain't' appears in Jenny's language.

The use of the present tense

A common feature of spoken narratives is the use of present tense even when describing past events. This is sometimes referred to as the historic present. It creates a sense of immediacy. It has also been suggested that narratives which are mainly in the past tense can sometimes shift to the present tense at moments that are particularly significant for the narrative. Jenny uses this feature when she describes the way her family were woken up early in the morning.

Demonstrative adjectives

Jenny refers to 'them good slave days'. In standard English 'those' would be the form of the **demonstrative adjective**. When she refers to 'that driver' the use of the demonstrative adjective is typical of speech. It has a **deictic** function. The memories are obviously vivid in Jenny's mind as she pictures events. She speaks to her audience as though they share the memory and can see the situation she is describing. This is an effective way of making the audience feel the immediacy of what is being described.

Syntax

Jenny's syntax is more typical of speech than writing at times. Although this extract is a tidied-up version of an original spoken account with sentence boundaries clearly marked, the syntax still reflects spoken language. When Jenny says of her mother, 'she was cook', she just inserts this clause without connecting it tightly within the structure of the remainder of the utterance.

Ellipsis

The spoken style is marked by the way clause elements are often left unstated and understood: 'We didn't have no good beds, [we] just [had] scaffolds nailed up to the wall.'

Dialect

Some of Jenny's vocabulary reflects the fact that she lived in America. She uses 'sure' in a distinctively American way.

Vocabulary

The language that Jenny uses also reflects her age and when she lived. She uses vocabulary that reflects the period of slavery: 'driver', 'nigger'.

Spelling and pronunciation

Some words are spelled to suggest the accent with which Jenny speaks: 'git', ''tended', ''bout', 'gal'. These spellings suggest the way she pronounces some vowels and also reflect the way that she tends not to pronounce the 'a' at the start of words.

Determiners

Sometimes Jenny does not use **articles**: 'she was cook'.

Double negatives

Jenny uses this very common non-standard feature on several occasions: 'I don't recollect nothing', 'we didn't have no good beds'.

The next text is an extract from a book called *Twelve Years a Slave* (Derby and Miller, 1854) by Solomon Northup. The style of this text is quite different from Jenny's account and is much more 'written'. We are going to use it to develop the skills of recasting source texts to create a spoken voice.

Text E: Solomon Northup

The only respite from constant labor the slave has through the whole year, is during the Christmas holidays. Epps allowed us three – others allow four, five and six days, according to the measure of their generosity. It is the only time to which they look forward with any interest or pleasure. They are glad when night comes, not only because it brings them a few hours repose, but because it brings them one day nearer Christmas. It is hailed with equal delight by the old and the young; even Uncle Abram ceases to glorify Andrew Jackson, and Patsy forgets her many sorrows, amid the general hilarity of the holidays. It is the time of feasting, and frolicking, and fiddling – the carnival season with the children of bondage. They are the only days when they are allowed a little restricted liberty, and heartily indeed do they enjoy it.

Soloman Northup *Twelve Years a Slave* (Derby and Miller, 1854)

As an examination or coursework task you might choose to write the script for elements of a new educational website about slavery. Parts of the website will include spoken personal accounts of slavery performed by actors. You have to write the script for these first-person accounts. You have been given Text E, an extract from

Solomon Northup's book *Twelve Years a Slave*, to use as part of your source material. How should you go about your rewriting task?

Exercise 7 – Preparing to Transform: Analysing the Style of the Source

Before embarking on a rewriting task it is always worth considering what kind of rewriting is going to be necessary. You need to assess the style of the sources and think about what needs to be changed and transformed.

Look at Solomon's language style. In what ways is it different from what would be appropriate as a first-person spoken account?

Suggestions for Answer

Solomon Northup's style is unlike a first-person spoken account in four main ways:

1. The vocabulary is very formal and of a high register: 'respite', 'hailed', 'ceases'.
2. It adopts a distanced third-person perspective.
3. The sentences can be long with several clauses.
4. The language is standard English.

Before undertaking a textual transformation it is worth planning out the features that you are going to use. Think about the features of texts similar to the one you have been asked to produce. In this case we can use Jenny Proctor's account.

Make a list of the features of her language. Now you have a checklist of things to put in your transformation. They are also the kind of things you would want to quote and discuss if you have to write a commentary explaining how you created the voice of your character.

Exercise 8 – Writing Your Transformed Text

Transform Text E into a first-person account. Write a brief commentary explaining how you created the first-person spoken style.

Suggestions for an answer to this exercise may be found at the back of the book on page 84.

EXERCISE SUMMARY

When creating a spoken voice, insert some of the following as appropriate to the individual voice:

- Fillers such as 'er'
- Monitoring features such as 'you know' or 'sort of'
- Interaction features such as 'yes' or questions
- Features of dialect
- Spellings to suggest pronunciation
- Examples of ellipsis
- Use of present tense
- Colloquial and informal expressions
- Deliberate inexplicitness with phrases such as 'that sort of thing'

SUMMARY

In this chapter we have looked at:

- Transforming speech into writing
- Converting written language into a spoken style
- The differences between spoken and written language

This work should help you:

- Prepare for transforming spoken accounts in analytical and editorial tasks
- Create a spoken voice when you are asked to adopt a first-person style when carrying out writing tasks
- Analyse and compare texts

TRANSFORMING TEXTS FROM DIFFERENT TIMES

CHAPTER 4

INTRODUCTION

In this chapter we look at transforming older texts. We shall consider:

- Why we might want to transform older texts
- How we would need to change the language of older texts to make them accessible to a modern audience
- What other changes are necessary to make older texts relevant to contemporary audiences

We shall look at extracts from Shakespeare's tragedy of ambition *Macbeth*, and his so-called comedy *The Taming of the Shrew* which tries to teach men how to put women in their place! Initially we shall look at ways of translating older English into modern English. Then we will need to explore some bigger issues about restaging Shakespeare to make him relevant to today. How can we put on a play such as *The Taming of the Shrew* which has a wife-beater as a hero? This will help you think about major creative rewriting tasks in which you transform literary texts.

At the end of the chapter we shall look at nineteenth-century investigative journalism as an American journalist reports on the horrors of starvation during the Irish potato famine. We shall look at the editorial writing issues in using such source material for TV and radio documentary.

Throughout the chapter the focus will be on the writing issues you face when transforming older texts. At the same time, however, you will also be exploring how language has changed by transforming older texts into modern English.

WHY MIGHT WE WANT TO TRANSFORM OLDER TEXTS?

In a 1980s TV series *Shakespeare Lives*, the director Michael Bogdanov argued that Shakespeare was the greatest living playwright. His argument was that Shakespeare dealt with themes that still had contemporary relevance: money, power, sex and the territorial imperative. He argued that Shakespeare's plays were plays for today.

However, in an article published in the *Independent* in 2001, Susan Bassnett, Professor at the Centre for Translation and Comparative Cultural Studies at the University of Warwick, raised a problem:

'The problem with Shakespeare today is linguistic. The language has become obsolete, Shakespeare's jokes are meaningless, his witticisms miss their target. It isn't the actors' fault: all they can do is struggle to make sense of a language that might as well be Tibetan.'

One answer to our question about the need to transform older texts is that there is a language barrier. Because English has changed it may be necessary to transform the language of a text so that it becomes accessible to a modern audience.

SHAKESPEARE MADE EASY

Shakespeare Made Easy is a series in which a Shakespeare play is presented with the original text on the left-hand page and a modern version on the right-hand page.

Exercise 1

Read the extract from *Macbeth* below. Identify any language features you think may present difficulties for a twenty-first-century reader.

[*Forres. The Palace. Flourish. Enter* King Duncan, Malcolm, Donalbain, Lennox *and* Attendants.]

DUNCAN: Is execution done on Cawdor? Are not
           Those in commission yet returned?
MALCOLM: My liege,
           They are not yet come back. But I have spoke
           With one that saw him die: who did report
           That very frankly he confessed his treasons,
           Implored your highness' pardon, and set forth
           A deep repentance: nothing in his life
           Became him like the leaving it; he died
           As one that had been studied in his death,
           To throw away the dearest thing he owed
           As 'twere a careless trifle.
DUNCAN: There's no art
           To find the mind's construction in the face:
           He was a gentleman on whom I built
           An absolute trust.

[*Enter* Macbeth, Banquo, Ross, *and* Angus.]

O worthiest cousin!
The sin of my ingratitude even now
Was heavy on me. Thou art so far before,
That swiftest wing of recompense is slow
To overtake thee. Would thou hadst less deserved,
That the proportion both of thanks and payment
Might have been mine! only I have left to say,
More is thy due than more than all can pay.

Shakespeare, *Macbeth*

Exercise 2

Compare the *Shakespeare Made Easy* version of the same extract which you will find below. What changes have been made to the text to make the meaning more accessible?

[*The palace at Forres. A fanfare. Enter* King Duncan, Malcolm, Donalbain, Lennox *and* Attendants.]

DUNCAN: Has Cawdor been executed? Have the officers in charge returned?
MALCOLM: Your Majesty they have not yet come back. But I've spoken to someone who saw Cawdor die. He said he confessed his treasons very frankly, implored Your Highness's pardon, and showed sincere repentance. He died far more honourably than he lived, and seemed resolved to throw away his dearest possession, as if it had no value.
DUNCAN: You can never tell from a man's face what's going on in his mind. I trusted him completely.

[*Enter* Macbeth, Banquo, Ross, *and* Angus.]

Oh, worthiest cousin! I feel guilty of ingratitude. You have achieved so much so quickly that I cannot keep up with the debt I owe to you. I wish you had deserved less. Then my thanks and rewards might have got ahead. I can only say that more is due to you than I can ever repay.

Alan Durband, *Shakespeare Made Easy: Macbeth*,
reprinted by permission of Nelson Thornes, 1984

Suggestions for Answer to Exercises 1 and 2

Discourse changes

Shakespeare wrote his play in blank verse. He used a rhythm called **iambic pentameter**. This was a metre that employed ten syllables arranged into five feet, each of which contained an unstressed syllable followed by a stressed syllable. The *Shakespeare Made Easy* version of the text has not used iambic pentameters and has switched to prose.

There are also some style changes. 'I have spoken' is changed to 'I've spoken' which shifts the formality register of the text downwards.

Spelling and punctuation changes

In the *Shakespeare Made Easy* version capitalisation is used to signal address terms to the King (e.g. 'Your Majesty'). The 'O' is changed in spelling to 'Oh'. The presentation of the original text here does not require a great deal of change to its spelling. It may be the case that some texts you deal with do have quite different spelling systems that would need to be transformed in creating a modern version.

Lexical changes

Some more difficult phrases and archaic words have been translated. 'Those in commission' becomes 'officers'. The phrase 'My liege' is now an archaic form for referring to someone to whom we owe allegiance. Our modern address phrase 'Your Majesty' is used instead. The use of 'one' as an **indefinite pronoun** is clarified by its replacement 'someone'.

Semantic changes

Idiomatic expressions which have fallen out of use have been altered. The expression 'to do execution on' has been altered to a simple verb in the passive in the first line.

Metaphorical expressions are often altered to more literal ones. The metaphoric adjective 'deep' is replaced by 'sincere'. Duncan's metaphors linked to building and construction are removed. At the end of the section a spatial metaphor is retained in 'might have got ahead' but this is barely noticeable in comparison with 'That swiftest wing of recompense is slow/To overtake thee'.

Grammatical changes

Verb forms indicate differences between the English of the seventeenth century and of today. There is a change made to the form of a past participle. 'I have spoke' becomes 'spoken'. There is a change made in the past tense of the verb 'to have'. In the Shakespeare original this is written as 'hadst' with an **inflection** which marks the fact that this is a second-person singular verb 'thou hadst'. In the *Shakespeare Made Easy* version this inflection is removed.

An inflection is an ending that is added on to a word. Inflections are used to indicate grammatical features such as **plurality**, tense and person. Earlier forms of English are often marked by the use of inflections on the verb depending on the person being used. Very few inflections remain, by comparison, in modern English.

A change in the use of auxiliary verbs is made. In modern English the **perfect aspect** is created using the auxiliary 'to have' with the past participle to indicate an action that has taken place and has been completed. An example of this from the *Shakespeare Made Easy* version is when Duncan asks whether the officers have returned. In Shakespeare's times, some verbs, especially verbs of motion, used the verb 'to be'. This is seen when 'Are not . . . returned' becomes 'Have . . . returned' and 'are not yet come back' becomes 'have not yet come back'.

Sentence boundaries are changed. In earlier forms of English the punctuation system was rather different. The structure of ideas would be signalled by commas, semicolons, colons and full stops. Each of these would represent a different length of utterance. The effect was that generally sentence boundaries were longer. In lines 3 to 11 of the Shakespeare text there is just one full stop. The *Shakespeare Made Easy* equivalent has three sentences.

Change is made to word order. The adverbial of manner 'very frankly' is placed after the verb rather than before it.

Pronouns are often different in earlier texts. When Duncan addresses Macbeth he uses the second-person singular **subject** pronoun 'thou'. The **object** pronoun 'thee' and the **possessive adjective** 'thy' also appear. These forms are archaic in modern English where there is no distinction between singular and plural in the second person. The *Shakespeare Made Easy* version uses only subject and object second-person pronouns, both of which take the form 'you'.

Cohesion changes

Some changes are made to the textual cohesion patterns. The pronoun 'him' is replaced by the proper noun 'Cawdor'. This makes the text more explicit. It also changes the nature of the textual cohesion. Instead of an example of grammatical cohesion where a pronoun is substituted for a noun to which it links back, lexical repetition is used to maintain the cohesive tie. This might be seen as a way of making the text more explicit and easy to follow.

Are all the changes discussed above simply to do with modernising the text? It could be argued that the style shifts, changes to cohesion patterns and the reduction of figurative language are to do with the complexity of the writing and its ideas rather than its period. The *Shakespeare Made Easy* series has a school audience in mind so its transformation may not be based simply on making the language contemporary. The text has been transformed with an eye on more than one aspect of its context. It has been transformed to suit a modern audience and one that also finds the ideas and general language level of Shakespeare difficult.

Exercise 3

Rewrite the extract below so that it could be used in the *Shakespeare Made Easy* version of the play.

At the beginning of the play Macbeth has been involved in a successful battle. On his way back from the battlefield he comes across three strange women. They foretell his future. They tell him that he will become the Thane of Cawdor and later King of Scotland. When he returns to the court the King rewards his success in battle by making him Thane of Cawdor. The prophecy is coming true. The following is the letter that Macbeth sends to his wife telling her about his meeting with the three witches and their prophecy.

They met me in the day of success: and I have learned by the perfectest report, they have more in them than mortal knowledge. When I burned in desire to question them further, they made themselves air, into which they vanished. Whiles I stood rapt in the wonder of it, came missives from the king, who all-hailed me 'Thane of Cawdor;' by which title, before, these weird sisters saluted me, and referred me to the coming on of time, with 'Hail, king that shalt be!' This have I thought good to deliver thee, my dearest partner of greatness, that thou mightst not lose the dues of rejoicing, by being ignorant of what greatness is promised thee. Lay it to thy heart, and farewell.

There is no commentary on this exercise.

GETTING THE REFERENCES

So far we have explored how the language of older texts needs to be adapted to make them accessible to a modern audience. However, understanding a text is not only about understanding the literal meanings of words. Words also carry connotational and cultural meanings. Texts are full of **allusions** and can make very demanding assumptions about the audience's cultural knowledge.

Think about a favourite television programme of yours and imagine trying to explain it to someone who understands the English language but has absolutely no experience of modern English culture. When we read a text from the past we often lack the cultural knowledge and frameworks that the author could assume in the audience. If we are going to transform a text for a modern audience we need to pay attention not only to the linguistic changes but also to the cultural references.

TRANSFORMING SHAKESPEARE'S *THE TAMING OF THE SHREW*

Shakespeare's play *The Taming of the Shrew* is a romance comedy. The typical plot in this genre revolves around young lovers trying to get together – the perfect subject for a modern teenage audience.

In the play all the young men are in love with Bianca Minola. Unfortunately her father Baptista has decreed that they will not be allowed to court her until her elder sister is married. The problem is that the elder sister Kate is a shrew and no one wants to marry her. A shrew was the label used for women who were seen as bad-tempered, complaining and unwilling to submit to men's wishes.

The play has been used recently as the basis for the teen comedy film *10 Things I Hate About You*. In the film the characters and settings of the play are translated to a modern American high school setting. In this film the language of the play has been abandoned: only characters and plot elements remain.

It would also be possible to make a film version of the play using a modern college setting while still staying close to the speeches of the original. In our transformation we are going to take more liberties with the language than if we were preparing a *Shakespeare Made Easy* version. We are also going to need to think about how we can update the cultural references to make what Shakespeare wrote comprehensible to a twenty-first-century audience with its web of cultural knowledge and savvy.

Shakespeare's play *The Taming of the Shrew* opens with the arrival in Padua of a young man Lucentio and his servant Tranio. They are the typical comic pairing of the stupid master and the clever servant – something like P.G. Wodehouse's Jeeves and Wooster and the reverse of Blackadder and Baldrick.

In Lucentio's first speech he announces that he has come to Padua to attend college and be a student. He cannot wait to start studying and pours out a list of all the things he wants to do:

> Here let us breathe, and haply institute
> A course of learning and ingenious studies. . . .
> And therefore, Tranio, for the time I study,
> Virtue and that part of philosophy
> Will I apply that treats of happiness
> By virtue specially to be achiev'd.

Tranio is horrified by Lucentio's attitude to college. He worries that Lucentio will end up stuck in a library with his nose in a book – and here they are: two young men in a new town, away from Lucentio's parents and with plenty of money from Lucentio's father! In his response Tranio tells Lucentio that he is pleased he is so keen to get on with his studies, but pleads with his master that they should make sure that their studies are practical and enjoyable. His motto is to study by doing things, and to do things that will be fun.

> *Mi perdonate*, gentle master mine,
> I am in all affected as yourself,
> Glad that you thus continue your resolve
> To suck the sweets of sweet *philosophy*.
> Only, good master, while we do admire
> This virtue and this moral discipline,
> Let's be no stoics nor no stocks, I pray;
> Or so devote to Aristotle's checks
> As Ovid be an outcast quite abjur'd.
> Balk *logic* with acquaintance that you have,
> And practise *rhetoric* in your common talk;
> *Music* and *poesy* use to quicken you;
> The *mathematics* and the *metaphysics*,
> Fall to them as you find your stomach serves you;
> No profit grows where is no pleasure ta'en;
> In brief, sir, study what you most affect.
>
> Shakespeare, *The Taming of the Shrew*

In this passage Tranio names seven subjects which have been placed in italics and underlined. The difficulty for a modern audience is that these subjects come from a different educational system. To transform this for a modern audience we would need to change the references to school subjects and update them for the twenty-first century.

Exercise 4

Choose seven subjects that your school or college offers. Write a speech to persuade a modern Lucentio to learn by putting his studies into practice and having a good time.

Here is a possible way of starting.

> Master, I am delighted you still want to go to college and agree with you absolutely that you should reap all the benefits of a Leisure and Tourism course. And while we're studying the popularity of theme parks where better to see this ourselves than in Disneyland Paris?

There is no further commentary on this exercise.

In the play a husband is eventually found for Kate. The other men who are in love with Bianca begin to compete for her hand in marriage.

The speech below is made by the character Gremio to Bianca's father. Gremio is an old man who would like to marry the young Bianca. In the play he is mocked because of the age gap between them and the unsuitability of the match. Gremio is trying to persuade Bianca's father that he is very wealthy and this makes him a suitable husband. In this speech Shakespeare expects the audience to understand allusions to Tyrian tapestry, cushions from Turkey and valances from Venice. These allusions all suggest great richness and quality. Gremio is trying to show off his possessions – the proper nouns here act almost as brand names.

> First, as you know, my house within the city
> Is richly furnished with plate and gold:
> Basins and ewers to lave her dainty hands;
> My hangings all of Tyrian tapestry;
> In ivory coffers I have stuff'd my crowns;
> In cypress chests my arras counterpoints,
> Costly apparel, tents, and canopies,
> Fine linen, Turkey cushions boss'd with pearl,
> Valance of Venice gold in needle-work,
> Pewter and brass, and all things that belong
> To house or housekeeping.

It is easy for a modern audience to get the general gist of this speech: Gremio's house is full of ornate decorations and high-quality possessions. However, we have probably not got the same impression of the rather heavy and overwhelming style of the house as Shakespeare's audience would have done. The allusions and indeed the items do not convey the same social messages to us as they would have done to someone in Shakespeare's audience. In our transformed version of the play we need to convey the idea that Gremio's house reflects the taste and possessions of a much older man hopelessly out of touch with what a young woman would find fashionable and desirable.

Exercise 5

Write a speech in prose for Gremio in which he tries to show off his wealth and possessions.

Try to list and describe modern household items and brand names to convey great richness and quality.

You could start by having Gremio promise Bianca a mobile phone. How could you make him describe it proudly while still revealing that he is offering something desperately out of date and that she would be embarrassed to use?

There is no further commentary on this exercise.

'BRUSH UP YOUR SHAKESPEARE'

This is the title of a song in a musical version of *The Taming of the Shrew* called *Kiss Me Kate*. Shakespeare's plays are sometimes transformed in very radical ways. They can shift genres from play to musical. Another way of transforming the text is to change its setting. This is often done to make the play seem 'relevant'. Theatrical and film performances sometimes use costume to make points about the play. Michael Bogdanov used modern military costume in his *Wars of the Roses* production of *Henry V* to make points about aggressive British militarism in the 1980s and the value of foreign wars to keep a nation united.

Another radical transformation is when the play is completely reset and rescripted. *Othello* has been transformed into a television drama about a black police officer working for the Metropolitan Police. *The Taming of the Shrew* was used as the basis for the American teen high school film comedy *10 Things I Hate About You*. In some ways all that remains is the plot of the original text.

This type of transformation might solve the problems of linguistic and cultural barriers to understanding Shakespeare, but is what we have got the Shakespeare text or something completely new?

In the article referred to at the beginning of this chapter, Susan Bassnett calls for new versions of Shakespeare:

> What we need are good English translators to take Shakespeare in hand and liberate him for a new generation. We need the Seamus Heaneys, Tony Harrisons, Timberlake Wertenbakers and Liz Locheads to get a grip on Shakespeare and wrestle him into beautiful modern English.

Tony Harrison has produced a modern English version of the medieval Mystery Plays. His versions are not simply paraphrases of the originals so that we can understand what appears to be a foreign language. He has produced new texts that try to be true to the creative spirit and nature of the originals. This cannot be done by a straightforward word-for-word translation. When we transform older texts we need to think about the audience and purpose of our transformation. It would be unfair to criticise *Shakespeare Made Easy* for losing the poetry if it is trying to provide only the literal sense. If we are seeking to write a script for dramatic performance then it may be necessary to transform in a more creative way so that it is true to the spirit rather than the letter of the text.

Exercise 6

Below is a brief outline of the plot of *Macbeth*. Key themes appear to be loyalty, ambition and ways of advancing yourself and protecting your position.

What contemporary situations could you use to make this story outline become relevant to a modern audience?

- Two lords, Macbeth and Banquo, return from a successful war
- They meet some strange women who prophesy that Macbeth will become a king and Banquo will have sons who will become kings
- Macbeth is promoted by the King
- His wife convinces him that this is a sign that the prophecy is coming true
- They decide to speed things along and kill the King
- Macbeth also kills Banquo so that his sons will not become kings
- Macbeth receives another prophecy warning him of the dangers of another lord, Macduff
- Macbeth kills Macduff's family
- Macbeth's wife loses her sanity and dies
- Macduff and the sons of the former King attack and defeat Macbeth

There is no commentary on this exercise.

TEXTS AND SOCIAL VALUES

When we transform a text for a modern audience there is a third dimension that we need to consider: **ideology**. Ideology is the manner of thinking characteristic of a particular group or class of people. Texts carry the social values of their writers and their times. *The Taming of the Shrew* is a comedy. One feature of this genre is the happy ending. Comedies often begin with some challenge or disruption to the world of the play. In *The Taming of the Shrew* the challenge is to the patriarchal family. The shrewish woman will not submit to men and marriage and so the basic unit of patriarchal society is under threat. By the end of the play the disruption is overcome and the society of the play is saved, perhaps having learned something and made some minor adaptations. Kate, the shrew of the title, is tamed and stops being a self-willed woman. She marries Petruchio and becomes an obedient wife because of the strategies he uses to tame her. The happy ending is 'happy' from the point of view of a male patriarchy: the independent woman resumes her place as subservient wife. Happy endings in comedies rely on the audience sharing the values and ideology of the society that is restored.

At the end of *The Taming of the Shrew* Kate has a long speech in which she explains how women should see their relationship to their husbands:

> Fie, fie! unknit that threatening unkind brow,
> And dart not scornful glances from those eyes,
> To wound thy lord, thy king, thy governor:
> . . . .
> Thy husband is thy lord, thy life, thy keeper,
> Thy head, thy sovereign; one that cares for thee,
> And for thy maintenance commits his body
> To painful labour both by sea and land,
> To watch the night in storms, the day in cold,
> Whilst thou liest warm at home, secure and safe;
> And craves no other tribute at thy hands
> But love, fair looks, and true obedience;
> Too little payment for so great a debt.
> Such duty as the subject owes the prince,
> Even such a woman oweth to her husband;
> . . . .
> I am asham'd that women are so simple
> To offer war where they should kneel for peace,
> Or seek for rule, supremacy, and sway,
> When they are bound to serve, love, and obey.
> Why are our bodies soft, and weak, and smooth,
> Unapt to toil and trouble in the world,
> But that our soft conditions and our hearts
> Should well agree with our external parts?

It is questionable whether a modern audience would find this a happy ending. During the play Kate has been made to succumb to a man's rule by a systematic process of starvation, sleep deprivation and psychological tyranny.

How might you transform this text to suit a modern audience with different values? There are a number of possibilities:

- Cut the speech and remove some of the extreme imagery
- Perform it in ways which reveal that Kate means it sarcastically, and is far from tamed
- Rewrite the ending of the play to show that Kate and Petruchio are equals

These are major textual transformations and begin to move the play further and further away from its historical context and the original text. There is more discussion of this kind of transformation in Chapter 5, 'Transforming Literary Genres'.

SUMMARY

In addition to simply translating and modernising the language of older texts, we have now considered some other issues about how to transform older texts:

- Do we need to update cultural allusions and references so that a modern audience will get the point?
- Do we need to modify a text's value messages to make it acceptable to a modern audience?
- Do we need to transform the settings of older texts to make them relevant to today's audiences?
- What are we gaining or losing by such transformations?

USING OLDER TEXTS AS SOURCES FOR WRITING TASKS

Sometimes we need to use older texts as sources for our own original or editorial writing. This means we will need to make decisions about how to transform the language to fit the new context. Consider the following situation:

You have been given a task to write the script for a radio documentary about the Irish Potato Famine in the nineteenth century. The programme is to contain exposition that will be read by a narrator and first-person eyewitness accounts. During your research for your writing you have found the following account that was written by the American journalist Elihu Burritt in 1847. In this text he explains the sights he came across as he travelled through west Cork. The source has lots of potential for the documentary, but it could not be read out in the documentary in the form it is now. How might you need to edit and transform the piece for its new use?

Exercise 7

Read Burritt's account. Identify the vocabulary of this text which you think needs adaptation to be suitable for the programme.

You may want to think about examples where the meaning could be made more accessible to a modern audience and the language less formal.

We entered a stinted den by an aperture about three feet high, and found one or two children lying asleep with their eyes open in the straw. Such, at least, was their appearance, for they scarcely winked while we were before them. The father came in and told his pitiful story of want, saying that not a morsel of food had they tasted for 24 hours. He lighted a wisp of straw and showed us one or two more children lying in another nook of the cave. Their mother had died, and he was obliged to leave them alone during most of the day, in order to glean something for their subsistence. We were soon among the most wretched habitations that I had yet seen, far worse than Skibbereen. Many of them were flat-roofed hovels, half-buried in the earth, or built up against the rocks, and covered with rotten straw, seaweed or turf. In one which was scarcely seven feet square, we found five persons prostrate with the fever, and apparently near their end. A girl about sixteen, the very picture of despair, was the only one left who could administer any relief; and all she could do was to bring water in a broken pitcher to slake their parched lips. As we proceeded up a rocky hill overlooking the sea we encountered new sights of wretchedness. Seeing a cabin standing somewhat by itself in a hollow, and surrounded by a moat of green filth, we entered it with some difficulty, and found a single child about three years old lying on a kind of shelf, with its little face resting upon the edge of the board and looking steadfastly out of the door as if for its mother. It never moved its eyes as we entered, but kept them fixed towards the entrance. It is doubtful whether the poor thing had a mother or father left to her; but it is more doubtful still whether those eyes would have relaxed their vacant gaze if both of them had entered at once with anything that could tempt the palate in their hands. No words can describe this peculiar appearance of the famished children. Never have I seen such bright, blue, clear eyes looking so steadfastly at nothing.

Elihu Burritt, *A Journal of a Visit to Skibbereen and its Neighbourhood*, 1847

Suggestions for Answer

In many respects this text could be used as it is. However, there are certain aspects of the language that would be difficult for modern listeners to process:

- There is some vocabulary that is quite complex or even rather old-fashioned
- Another aspect of the text which needs some attention is the grammar. The text was produced originally as a written text. This means that the text could be

transformed to reflect the different grammar of spoken language and be made more personal

1. The words 'stinted' and 'aperture' are perhaps not entirely clear to a modern audience and could be reduced in formality. They could be changed to 'cramped' and 'opening'.
2. A simpler synonym could be given for 'obliged' which could be replaced by 'had'.
3. The word 'pitcher' might be retained to give a sense of the nineteenth-century context but the expression 'slake their parched lips' could be changed to '*wet* their parched lips'.
4. The formal and polysyllabic words 'proceeded' and 'encountered' could be shortened and transformed so that the sentence reads 'As we *carried on* up a rocky hill overlooking the sea we *came across* new sights of wretchedness'. The use of **multi-word verbs** here helps create a more spoken voice.
5. The words 'looking steadfastly' could be replaced by '*staring fixedly*' to clarify exactly how the child is staring. If this change is made, it would be helpful to change the second use of 'steadfastly' also to retain Burritt's deliberate use of repetition.
6. The expression 'left to her' is euphemistic. This could be transformed to be clearer by being reworded as 'It is doubtful whether the poor thing's mother or father *were still alive*'.
7. The expression 'tempt the palate' is one which could be made more plain. It could be transformed as 'if both of them had entered at once with anything in their hands that could make her *want to eat*'.

As well as transforming the vocabulary of the text, it would be helpful to adapt the grammar to make the language more easily processed by a modern listener.

Exercise 8

Below you will see some of the sentences that could be transformed. Rewrite the sentences to make them shorter, more personal and in conventional modern word order. Comment linguistically on the changes you have made.

1. The father came in and told his pitiful story of want, saying that not a morsel of food had they tasted for twenty-four hours.
2. Many of them were flat-roofed hovels, half-buried in the earth, or built up against the rocks, and covered with rotten straw, seaweed or turf.
3. A girl about sixteen, the very picture of despair, was the only one left who could administer any relief; and all she could do was to bring water in a broken pitcher to slake their parched lips.

Suggestions for Answer

The kinds of change that might be made are:

- The shortening of sentences and simplification of their structure
- Making sentences more personal and active in style
- Making word order modern and conventional

Here are some possible ways to rewrite the text. This is not the kind of activity where there are right answers. You may disagree with some of the linguistic choices made below. When you are asked to comment on your linguistic choices in examination tasks, you are being asked to justify your way of writing because there are different ways you can approach the same task, creating quite different results depending on what you want to convey.

> 1. The father came in and told his pitiful story of want, saying that *they had not tasted a morsel of food for twenty-four hours.*

In this case the word order has been altered. The inverted clause order of object ('morsel') verb and subject 'they' has been changed to a more conventional subject verb object sequence.

> 2. Many of them were flat-roofed hovels, half-buried in the earth. *Others* were built up against the rocks, and covered with rotten straw, seaweed or turf.

The three-clause compound sentence of the original has been changed into a simple sentence and a two-clause compound sentence.

> 3. A girl about sixteen, the very picture of despair, was the only one left who could administer any relief. *All* she could do was to bring water in a broken pitcher to slake their parched lips.

The sentence length and complexity have been reduced by the removal of the co-ordinating conjunction 'and'.

Exercise 9

Below you will see some more sentences that could be transformed. Rewrite the sentences to make them shorter, more personal and in conventional modern word order. Comment linguistically on the changes you have made.

Suggestions for an answer to this exercise may be found at the back of the book on page 85.

---

4. Seeing a cabin standing somewhat by itself in a hollow, and surrounded by a moat of green filth, we entered it with some difficulty, and found a single child about three years old lying on a kind of shelf, with its little face resting upon the edge of the board and looking steadfastly out of the door as if for its mother.
5. It is doubtful whether the poor thing had a mother or father left to her; but it is more doubtful still whether those eyes would have relaxed their vacant gaze if both of them had entered at once with anything that could tempt the palate in their hands.
6. Never have I seen such bright, blue, clear eyes looking so steadfastly at nothing.

SUMMARY

In this chapter we have:

- Explored ways of rewriting and adapting older texts for modern audiences
- Considered different degrees of transformation of older texts, from linguistic translation to complete rewriting and resetting
- Examined how older texts draw on networks of cultural allusions that might need to be transformed so that a modern audience does not miss the point
- Explored how to deal with the way texts contain social values and ideologies from their time of writing which may not be acceptable now

This work should help you:

- Transform and rewrite older literary texts for modern audiences
- Comment on the distinctive features of earlier forms of English
- Edit older sources for use within your own new pieces of writing

TRANSFORMING LITERARY GENRES

CHAPTER 5

INTRODUCTION

In Chapter 4 we began to look at the way theatrical and film productions of Shakespeare's plays transformed the original play quite radically to make it accessible to new audiences. The focus was on how older texts could be brought up to date. In this chapter we are going to look at how literary texts can be transformed in other ways.

One way that literary texts are transformed or rewritten is by the production of versions that tell the story from a different point of view. Jean Rhys' *Wide Sargasso Sea* transforms Charlotte Brontë's *Jane Eyre* by focusing on the character Bertha Mason who in the original novel is imprisoned in the attic of Mr Rochester's house. Tom Stoppard's play *Rosencrantz and Guildenstern are Dead* takes two minor characters from *Hamlet* and puts them centre stage. Stoppard explores the nature of the lives of these bit-part characters who seem to be the playthings of others. A similar transformation strategy is where writers choose to write sequels or new sections to throw new light on the text.

Literary texts are also transformed for people who are learning English as a foreign language. There are many versions of classic texts which have been abridged or simplified for such readers. There are interesting analytical or creative projects to be undertaken comparing versions or writing simplified texts.

Another way in which texts are transformed is by altering their medium and genre. Many novels are abridged for reading on radio or as audiobooks. *The Taming of the Shrew* has been changed into a musical called *Kiss Me Kate*. Many literary texts have been transformed into films or television programmes. What all these transformations show is that there is big business in rewriting texts. It is possible to draw on the success and reputation of an already existing story by transforming it for a new audience and market.

In this chapter we are going to explore how fictional and non-fiction prose texts are converted into screenplays for films.

FEVER PITCH: FROM PROSE AUTOBIOGRAPHY TO FILM

The following text is an extract from Nick Hornby's autobiographical book *Fever Pitch*. The book is about his obsession with football and especially Arsenal. In his introduction Hornby says the book is an exploration of what it is like to be a football fan and what football can mean to people. In this section he describes watching the final game of the season in which Arsenal beat Liverpool to win the championship.

Exercise 1

What difficulties does this extract present for someone writing the screenplay for a film version of the book?

Text A: *Fever Pitch* – Prose Text

I got excited when we scored right at the beginning of the second half and I got excited again about ten minutes from time when Thomas had a clear chance and hit it straight at Grobbelaar but Liverpool seemed to be growing stronger and to be creating chances at the end and finally with the clock in the corner of the TV screen showing that the ninety minutes had passed I got ready to muster a brave smile for a brave team. 'If Arsenal are to lose the Championship having had such a lead at one time, it's somewhat poetic justice that they have got a result on the last day even though they're not to win it,' said co-commentator David Pleat as Kevin Richardson received treatment for an injury with the Kop already celebrating. 'They'll see that as scant consolation I should think, David,' replied Brian Moore. Scant consolation indeed, for all of us.

Richardson finally got up, ninety-two minutes gone now, and even managed a penalty area tackle on John Barnes; then Lukic bowled the ball out to Dixon, Dixon on, inevitably, to Smith, a brilliant Smith flick-on and suddenly in the last minute of the last game of the season, Thomas was through, on his own with a chance to win the Championship for Arsenal. 'It's up for grabs now,' Brian Moore yelled; and even then I found that I was reining myself in, learning from recent lapses in hardened skepticism, thinking, well, at least we came close at the end there, instead of thinking, please Michael, please Michael, please put it in, please God let him score. And then he was turning a somersault and I was flat out on the floor and everybody in the living room jumped on top of me. Eighteen years all forgotten in a second.

Nick Hornby, *Fever Pitch*, Indigo, 1993

Suggestions for Answer

If we focus on the sequence above we can see the kinds of problem facing a writer trying to convert this into a film script.

- The bulk of the action in this sequence is actually the football showing on television. A film of someone watching a football match is not going to be very exciting or dramatic!
- There is really only one character (although others are present) and he is watching the football with some concentration. This means the scene will lack conflict and drama.
- The main interest of the sequence is interior as Hornby recounts his feelings. We are told when he got excited and how he began to try to put a brave face on if Arsenal should fail to win the championship. He also comments on how he has recently begun to be optimistic about Arsenal's chances, only to be badly let down. Now he deliberately avoids any hope or optimism. Where a novel or autobiography can use the narrative to explain and explore in addition to reported speech, film has to rely on dialogue and action to convey feelings and ideas.
- There is very little dialogue and Hornby relies on a past tense first-person narrative. There is some direct speech as Hornby quotes what the TV commentators say. Hornby also conveys thought when he says, 'well, at least we came close at the end there'. He does not put this in inverted commas as would be the convention with the representation of direct thought. What he has done distances the reader further from direct access to the thoughts which are refracted through his narrative.

In writing the screenplay Hornby needed to increase the dramatic nature of the sequence and to exteriorise feelings.

Fever Pitch was transformed into a highly successful film. In the introduction to the screenplay Hornby writes about the problems of transforming his autobiographical text into a film. The book is made up of a series of accounts of matches from 1968 to 1991. Through these accounts Hornby explores his fascination with football and his own growing up and development. This led to the first problem in transforming book into film: the time scale of the narrative was too long. The film therefore concentrates on one season.

Hornby also changed the book by moving away from its autobiographical focus and creating a fictional central character, Paul. This also enabled him to develop a range of supporting characters and further plot elements. In the book it was possible to explore the interior life of the one character. In the film it was necessary to introduce a wider range of characters and develop more plot strands for dramatic interest. In the film the character of Sarah is introduced as love-interest and Hornby is able to show the way Paul's obsession with football almost ruins his relationships. Hornby has said that it was necessary to take liberties on a large scale to effect the transition from one genre to another.

The sequence below is the written film script version of the extract you read on page 52. Paul is with a character created for the film. Steve is Paul's friend and another Arsenal fan. This screenplay gives the dialogue, guides the actors' performances and provides suggestions for the way the film should be directed. As well as the scenes reprinted here there are also some scenes featuring Paul's girlfriend Sarah, who is looking to him to patch up their relationship, which has faltered because of his obsession with football. The scenes with Sarah have not been reproduced here.

Exercise 2

How is the film script presented and laid out?

How does the script try to visualise the scenes as performed and filmed?

How has Hornby written the screenplay to create visible drama, conflict and narrative tension for the film?

How has Hornby created the spoken voices of his characters?

Text B: *Fever Pitch* – Screenplay

Scene 107 INT PAUL'S FLAT. EVENING.

PAUL: I'll just hear what they've got to say.
STEVE: We're doing OK, aren't we?
PAUL: What's the use of OK? We might as well be losing eight-nil.
STEVE: I don't think that's really true, Paul, is it? I'd say that if you want to win a game two-nil, you've got more chance if it's nil-nil at half-time than you have if you're eight goals down. Do you see where I'm coming from?
PAUL: You're living in cloud-cuckoo-land. Join the real world.
STEVE: In the real world it's nil-nil at half-time.
PAUL: Might as well be eight-nil.
STEVE: Jesus, Paul. You need medical help. You've got some kind of disease that turns people into miserable bastards. Anyway, are you staying?
PAUL: No.

[*He makes no move to leave.*]

PAUL: I'll just watch the first couple of minutes of the second half.

[*TV footage of the game. Smith scores for Arsenal. Reaction shots of* STEVE *and* PAUL (STEVE *ecstatic,* PAUL *excited despite himself*), ROBERT *and his* MOTHER, *etc.*

Liverpool players surround the referee, trying to persuade him to consult with the linesman.]

PAUL: He's going to disallow it. You watch. Bloody typical. I'll bet you any money you like.

TV COMMENTATOR: The goal stands. Liverpool nil, Arsenal one.

PAUL: Isn't that just like Arsenal? They need two so they score one, just to get us all going.

STEVE: What, you wanted them to score the second one before the first one?

[*Dissolve.* PAUL, *still standing by the door, and* STEVE *look at their watches nervously. Cut to TV footage of the game.*

Michael Thomas gets the ball, shoots from close range straight at Grobbelaar.]

SCENE 108 INT ROBERT'S MOTHER'S HOUSE. EVENING

[ROBERT'S MOTHER *covers her face with her hands.*]

ROBERT: I told you! He's useless!

SCENE 109 INT PAUL'S FLAT. EVENING

PAUL: That's it! I've had enough. I'm off.

STEVE: Good. Fucking good riddance.

PAUL: Are you coming?

STEVE: No.

PAUL: It's my flat.

STEVE: You try getting me out of it.

[PAUL *still makes no move to leave.*]

SCENE 113 INT PAUL' S FLAT. EVENING

[PAUL *is still standing by the door.*]

PAUL: We shouldn't even have turned the TV on tonight. What did we think would happen? I don't reckon I'll be able to carry on after this. I won't be able to pick myself up. To get this close. . . . Why did I listen to you?

STEVE: Me?

PAUL: You said we had a chance.

STEVE: Well, we did. Do.

PAUL: You're pathetic. We're just about in injury time already. I might start supporting a team that never wins. Orient or someone. Then at least you know where you stand. You wouldn't lay yourself open to situations like this.

continued

[*The buzzer goes.*]

PAUL: Can you believe that?

STEVE: You're on your way out. See what they want when you're down there.

[PAUL *doesn't move. The buzzer goes again. TV footage of the game: Kevin Richardson is being treated for an injury. During the break in play, we see McMahon and Barnes exhorting their Liverpool team mates; McMahon makes his one-minute gesture.*]

PAUL: This is awful. It's like the end of the word or something.

TV COMMENTATOR: And if Arsenal are to lose, having had such a lead at one time . . .

[*The buzzer goes again.*]

. . . then it's somewhat poetic justice that they should get a result here tonight.

STEVE: Oh, shut up, Pleat.

[*The buzzer goes again, for the longest duration yet.* PAUL *leaps for the window, opens it and yells out into the street.*]

PAUL: Please, please, please, please, please, just fucking . . . FUCK OFF. You have arrived during the worst sixty seconds of my life and I really don't want to see you.

SCENE 115 INT PAUL'S FLAT. EVENING

[PAUL *shuts the window and goes back to his sentry position on the door.*]

PAUL: I ask you, what kind of berk would do that? You could just about forgive an alien visitor from the planet Zarg, but even then you'd . . .

[PAUL *suddenly realizes who the alien visitor might have been, and races out of the door.*]

STEVE: Where are you going? You're mad. You might miss something.

SCENE 116 EXT STREET. EVENING

[PAUL *opens the door – no* SARAH. *He stands for a moment, curses, slams the door shut.*]

SCENE 117 TV FOOTAGE OF THE GAME

> [*Richardson is up on his feet. Adams skies the ball, Richardson rescues the situation, knocks the ball back to Lukic.*]

SCENE 118 INT STAIRS IN PAUL'S FLAT. EVENING

> [PAUL *hares up the stairs like a man possessed.*]

SCENE 119 TV FOOTAGE OF THE GAME

> [*Lukic to Dixon, and Dixon's long ball to Smith.*]

SCENE 120 INT STAIRS TO PAUL'S FLAT. EVENING

> [PAUL *is nearly at the door.*]

STEVE [(OOV) *hysterically*]: Pauuul!

SCENE 121 INT PAUL'S FLAT. EVENING

> [*TV footage of the game — Smith to Thomas.*
>
> *Cut to Paul's flat — the door of the flat bursts open and* PAUL *enters almost horizontally, knocking* STEVE *to the ground.*
>
> *Cut to TV footage — Thomas scores for Arsenal in the last minute of the game.* PAUL *and* STEVE *stare at the screen disbelieving for a moment, and then start shrieking.*]

PAUL/STEVE: Yeeeeees!

SCENE 122 INT PAUL'S MOTHER'S HOUSE. EVENING

> [*Reaction shot of Paul's* MOTHER, *delighted.*]

SCENE 123 INT ROBERT'S MOTHER'S HOUSE. EVENING

> [*Reaction shot of* ROBERT *and his* MUM, *ecstatic.*]

ROBERT'S MUM: Micky Thomas! Micky Thomas!

continued

> SCENE 125   INT PAUL'S FLAT. EVENING
>
> [STEVE *and* PAUL *are still lying on the ground intertwined.*]
>
> PAUL: How much injury time is there?
> STEVE: We've had two minutes already.
> PAUL: You watch. They'll go straight up the other end and score. You see if
>   they don't.
>
> Nick Hornby, *Fever Pitch – The Screenplay*, Indigo, 1997

Suggestions for Answer

The presentation of the script

The screenplay is not the same as a storyboard, which would involve drawings of the planned shots and full description of the intended camera and editing work. In a screenplay we are given the dialogue with indications of the visualisation.

The layout of the text is obviously different. The text is broken down into numbered scenes which consist of certain elements.

- Each scene begins with a number (e.g. 121)
- Then it is noted whether this scene is an Interior (INT) or Exterior scene (EXT) or makes use of film footage
- There then follows a brief note of where and when the scene is set: PAUL'S FLAT. EVENING
- The scene-setting details are in block capitals
- Dialogue is introduced by the character's name and a colon. Inverted commas are not used
- Italicised text is used to give stage instructions about movement, actions and noises

Filming and acting details

The script tries to visualise the scene. It gives suggestions to the actors about how they should behave and act. The script also gives hints to the director about some major elements of the shooting of the scene.

At the beginning of each section the abbreviations INT and EXT are used. We are given further details of time and location.

There is also some use of film jargon as the screenplay indicates the way it imagines certain shots being carried out and the way the film should move from scene to scene:

- *Cut*: an instantaneous switch to another shot
- *Reaction shot*: a shot used to show how a character reacts to something that has just happened or has just been said
- *Dissolve*: a method of switching from one shot to another. The first shot gradually disappears while the second shot gradually appears on screen
- *OOV (out of view)*: indicates the dialogue spoken by a character who is not on screen

There are also brief descriptions, similar to stage instructions, of what the characters do.

- The descriptions are italicised to show their different function
- They are written in the present tense ('He makes no move to leave') with some use of **progressives** as well ('Paul is still standing by the door.')
- The sentences are sometimes **minor** without a main verb and/or subject ('Steve ecstatic') to keep these descriptions short so that they do not interfere with the development of the dialogues
- Their content mainly describes characters' actions and their emotions which actors would need to convey in performances
- Adjectives and **adverbs** are used frequently (e.g. 'ecstatic' and 'hysterically') to convey characters' feelings and behaviour

Creating drama, conflict and narrative tension

Hornby has used two characters to enable him to exteriorise and express the emotions being felt and to create dramatic conflict. By having two characters Hornby can create dialogue and introduce conflict between them.

Hornby has taken the two opposing feelings he describes himself experiencing in the book and gives one to each of his two characters. Paul and Steve represent the two sides of Hornby himself: Paul is the pessimistic half while Steve is optimistic. Between them they express the feelings of the supporter: the unbearable desire of watching. The antagonism between the two characters explores the feelings and makes for interesting viewing. Hornby has been able to make his 'reining in' and 'hardened skepticism' concrete.

In scene 107 Hornby is able to play off the characters for comic effect. We laugh at the spiralling illogical pessimism of Paul and the increasing frustration of Steve. There is a mini-comic climax within the scene as Paul announces he can't stay but promptly makes no move to leave.

To increase further the tension Hornby cuts to other characters showing their reactions too. The cuts to Robert and to Paul's mother allow for greater visual interest and also for Hornby to ratchet up the tension each time we come back to Paul. Hornby uses a series of parallel scenes which end with Paul saying he can't bear it but still not leaving.

The person at the door was Sarah seeking a reconciliation. Hornby makes use of two plotlines and cuts between them to increase tension. During this part of the film Hornby cuts between Sarah and Paul to build up further dramatic conflict and excitement. We know who won the championship, but what will happen to Paul's relationship? Sarah's buzzing at the door also acts as another force pulling Paul away from the game. This provides yet more tension – we know that if he gives in and goes down, something important will happen. The sequences of Paul running up and down the stairs are rich in comic potential but also symbolise the way he is torn between two loves: Sarah and Arsenal.

The characters' speech

The language of the two characters is very interactive with lots of questions to create drama. Hornby also seeks to make the language as natural as possible.

- He indicates how the actors should speak the lines through his use of non-standard spellings, capitals and punctuation
- Sentences are short and often minor
- Vocabulary is colloquial. There is slang and swearing

Exercise 3

Nineteenth-century novels have been a very popular source of television and films scripts. This is due partly to their strong narratives, cast of characters and lively dialogue. Below is an extract from Jane Austen's novel *Sense and Sensibility*. Elinor and Marianne are two sisters. They are discussing Edward Ferrars to whom Elinor is attracted.

Transform this short sequence into a film script.

A suggestion for an answer to this exercise may be found at the back of the book on page 86.

Text C: *Sense and Sensibility* – Prose Text

'Of his sense and his goodness,' continued Elinor, 'no one can, I think, be in doubt, who has seen him often enough to engage him in unreserved conversation. The excellence of his understanding and his principles can be concealed only by that shyness which too often keeps him silent. You know enough of him to do justice to his solid worth. But of his minuter propensities as you call them you have from peculiar circumstances been kept more ignorant than myself. He and I have been at times thrown a good deal together, while you have been wholly engrossed on the most affectionate principle by my mother. I have seen a great deal of him, have studied his sentiments and heard his opinion on subjects of literature and taste; and, upon the whole, I venture to pronounce that his mind is well-informed, his enjoyment of books exceedingly great, his imagination lively, his observation just and correct, and his taste delicate and pure. His abilities in every respect improve as much upon acquaintance as his manners and person. At first sight, his address is certainly not striking; and his person can hardly be called handsome, till the expression

continued

of his eyes, which are uncommonly good, and the general sweetness of his countenance, is perceived. At present, I know him so well, that I think him really handsome; or, at least, almost so. What say you, Marianne?'

'I shall very soon think him handsome, Elinor, if I do not now. When you tell me to love him as a brother, I shall no more see imperfection in his face, than I now do in his heart.'

Elinor started at this declaration, and was sorry for the warmth she had been betrayed into, in speaking of him. She felt that Edward stood very high in her opinion. She believed the regard to be mutual; but she required greater certainty of it to make Marianne's conviction of their attachment agreeable to her. She knew that what Marianne and her mother conjectured one moment, they believed the next – that with them, to wish was to hope, and to hope was to expect. She tried to explain the real state of the case to her sister.

'I do not attempt to deny,' said she, 'that I think very highly of him – that I greatly esteem, that I like him.'

Marianne here burst forth with indignation –

'Esteem him! Like him! Cold-hearted Elinor! Oh! Worse than cold-hearted! Ashamed of being otherwise. Use those words again and I will leave the room this moment.'

Elinor could not help laughing. 'Excuse me,' said she, 'and be assured that I meant no offence to you, by speaking in so quiet a way, of my own feelings. Believe them to be stronger than I have declared; believe them, in short, to be such as his merit, and the suspicion – the hope of his affection for me may warrant, without imprudence or folly. But farther than this you must not believe. I am by no means assured of his regard for me. There are moments when the extent of it seems doubtful; and till his sentiments are fully known, you cannot wonder at my wishing to avoid any encouragement of my own partiality, by believing or calling it more than it is. In my heart I feel little – scarcely any doubt of his preference. But there are other points to be considered besides his inclination. He is very far from being independent. What his mother really is we cannot know; but, from Fanny's occasional mention of her conduct and opinions, we have never been disposed to think her amiable; and I am very much mistaken if Edward is not himself aware that there would be many difficulties in his way, if he were to wish to marry a woman who had not either a great fortune or high rank.'

Marianne was astonished to find how much the imagination of her mother and herself had outstripped the truth.

'And you really are not engaged to him!' said she. 'Yet it certainly soon will happen. But two advantages will proceed from this delay. *I* shall not lose you so soon, and Edward will have greater opportunity of improving that natural taste for your favourite pursuit which must be so indispensably necessary to your future felicity. Oh! if he should be so far stimulated by your genius as to learn to draw himself, how delightful it would be!'

SUMMARY

In this chapter on transforming literary texts we have looked at:

- Different ways literary texts are transformed and how you could use this for analytical investigations or writing tasks
- The issues involved when transforming prose fiction and non-fiction into a screenplay for a film
- The presentation and layout of screenplays
- The use of different characters to create conflict and drama
- The use of dialogue between different characters to exteriorise internal debates and conflicts
- The representation of natural speech
- The intercutting of plot strands to create tension

This work should help you:

- Deal with exercises comparing different versions of texts
- Write screenplays as a way of transforming literary texts for coursework

USING SOURCES AND COMBINING TEXTS

CHAPTER 6

INTRODUCTION

When writing we often need to make use of source materials or research materials. But how do we use source materials within a new text without plagiarising someone else's work and how do we combine them?

The first part of this chapter looks at the different ways you can make use of sources. It will remind you of some of the ways you have transformed texts earlier in this book. We shall then look at the problems when you are combining material from several different sources to write a new text and how to make sure your new piece of writing reads smoothly and does not end up like a Frankenstein's monster made up of badly fitting bits from all sorts of places.

We shall then look at a piece of investigative journalism about threats to the environment. We will be able to see how journalists carry out research and make use of sources in a new piece of writing. Finally, we will look at all the kinds of decision you need to make when putting together your own new text.

DIFFERENT WAYS OF USING SOURCES

When given a number of texts to use as the sources for your own writing it is necessary to think about what will be the most appropriate way to transform them as they become part of your own text. It is possible to think about using sources on a scale of how close to the original source the new text will be (Figure 6.1).

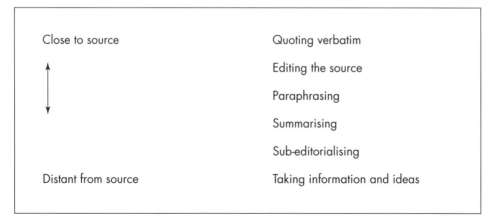

Figure 6.1 Different ways of using sources

1. Quoting Verbatim

In this situation you use the words from your source exactly as they are in the original.

Writing issues

You will need to signal that the text you are using is a quotation. You might do this by using quotation marks or italicising it. Another device you could use is to indent the quoted material more than the rest of the text. You will have noticed examples of these methods throughout this book.

You will also need to think about attributing the quotation. This might be done in an academic way by using a footnote at the foot of a page or at the end of a section or chapter.

In your text:

> The status of literary texts, then, is based ultimately on opinion, opinion which is usually underpinned by a long-standing reputation.[1]

At the end of the section or at the bottom of the page:

> 1 A. Beard, *How Texts Work*, London: Routledge, 2003, page 62.

Another method would be to put the details of the source after the quoted materials:

> It has been argued that 'The status of literary texts, then, is based ultimately on opinion, opinion which is usually underpinned by a long-standing reputation.' (Beard 2003: 62)

You should give details of the source in your Bibliography in the following style:

> Beard, A. (2003) *How Texts Work*, London: Routledge.

You might also use an introductory sentence to introduce the quotation. Key features here will be the description of the person quoted, the verb of saying used and any adverbs you choose to describe the verb. It is possible to vary the approach here from a quite neutral style to a dramatic style or one in which you convey a lot of attitudinal information. Here is an extract from the newspaper feature article discussed later in this chapter:

> The economic importance of oyster fishing was adversely compared with the large yachting industry. 'At the end of the day,' —— an editorial in *Yachting Monthly*, 'we are talking about a luxury delicacy against a type of paint developed to give us easier and safer sailing.'

The gap here is where a verb of saying was used. 'Wrote' would be neutral and fit the written source. 'Argued' would suggest that the writer endorses the view as rationally put forward. The actual choice was 'sniffed'. This suggests that the writer sees the view of the magazine to be rather self-important.

2. Editing the Source

This is another technique where you use the words of the original source as they are. This time you select some of the source and leave out other parts.

Writing issues

You will need to consider the same points as when you were planning to use a verbatim quotation. You will also need to think about how to signal that you have adapted your text. If you have omitted sections then you will need to indicate this using three dots (. . .) where text has been omitted. You should also put in a full stop if this takes you to the end of a sentence. Sometimes editing may affect the grammar of a sentence or make its references unclear. In this case you may use square brackets to add something, such as a pronoun or a verb ending, to make the edited version read fluently within your own text. If we quote the following extract from *How Texts Work* it is not clear what 'they' refers to:

> Within those two categories they have some qualities which are similar and some which are different.

To clarify this we could insert some square-bracketed information:

> Within those two categories [the advert and the poem] have some qualities which are similar and some which are different.

3. Paraphrase

Sometimes it will be appropriate to rewrite the text in almost a word-by-word fashion as in a translation. This might be where you have been required to present the text for a younger audience or for a reader who is learning English and requires a simplified text. There are several ways you might need to reword the text:

- Using simpler synonyms
- Adopting a less technical register
- Turning passive verbs into active verbs
- Converting longer, multi-clause sentences into shorter, possibly single-clause sentences

Examples of this close, detailed transformation were looked at in Chapter 2.

4. Summary

In this mode you try to reduce the text to its most important ideas. You will have to consider how many words you need to reduce the text by and then select your material accordingly. In this mode of rewriting you will need to judge whether the wording of the original text is the most economic way of presenting the information. You may even choose to use devices such as bullet points, lists, tables, timelines, flowcharts and diagrams.

5. Sub-editorial Writing

In newspapers, it is the journalist who writes an article. A sub-editor will then prepare the text for publication. They may choose to edit or rewrite sections of the original article. They will also, however, add elements to the article. These will include things such as:

1. A headline.
2. A sub-editorial introduction.
3. Subheadings.
4. A picture.
5. Captions.
6. Pull quotes (quotations extracted from the article and printed to stand out).

Most of these items numbered 1 to 6 are designed to summarise what an article is about so that it will communicate quickly even to those readers who merely scan it. These features are also written to make the article seem interesting and to tempt and hook a reader. As you combine texts into a new whole you may find it necessary to do the same. Table 6.1 on page 67 is a plan of an article layout with these six sub-editorial features put in.

Table 6.1 Plan of an article layout

<table>
<tr><td colspan="3">

1. Headline

This should be attention grabbing – dramatic with some witty use of language

</td></tr>
<tr><td colspan="3">

2. The sub-editorial introduction

– gives a summary of the article's content and its line of argument, e.g.:

Shaun O'Toole reveals the sub-editorial conventions for an article.

</td></tr>
<tr>
<td>

Main text main text main text
Main text main text main text
Main text main text main text

3. Subheading

Main text main text main text
Main text main text main text
Main text main text main text

</td>
<td>

Main text main text main text
Main text main text main text
Main text main text main text

4. A picture

</td>
<td>

Main text main text main text
Main text main text main text
Main text main text main text
Main text main text main text

3. Subheading

Main text main text main text
Main text main text main text

</td>
</tr>
<tr>
<td>

6. Pull quote

Quote a lively and eye-catching taster from the text

</td>
<td>

5. A caption

This should describe and interpret the significance of the picture

</td>
<td>

6. Pull quote

Quote a lively and eye-catching taster from the text

</td>
</tr>
<tr>
<td>

Main text main text main text
Main text main text main text
Main text main text main text
Main text main text main text
Main text main text main text
Main text main text main text

</td>
<td>

Main text main text main text
Main text main text main text
Main text main text main text
Main text main text main text
Main text main text main text
Main text main text main text

</td>
<td>

Main text main text main text
Main text main text main text
Main text main text main text
Main text main text main text
Main text main text main text
Main text main text main text

</td>
</tr>
</table>

6. Using the Source for Information

In some ways this is the biggest departure from using the language of your source text. Here you are simply using the text as a source of information. You are taking facts and figures or ideas which will be part of your own text. You will of course need to be careful about any bias in the original sources. By using sources this way you may transform them quite radically.

CASE STUDY 1 – WRITING ABOUT THE IRISH POTATO FAMINE

You may decide that for an original writing task you would like to write something on a historical subject that is a source of great interest to you. You could collect a set of source materials, for example, about the Irish Potato Famine of the nineteenth century. The materials are drawn from a variety of history books. Alternatively you could be presented with this kind of source material for an editorial or recasting exercise and given a writing brief.

You could choose or be set a variety of writing tasks:

1. To write the texts for display boards to be used in a museum which is staging an exhibition about the Famine.
2. To write the script for a radio drama-documentary about the Famine.
3. To write the text for a children's history book about the Famine.

Exercise 1

Which of the following ways of using your sources might you employ for each of tasks 1 to 3?

If you were taking information and ideas from your sources, how would you re-present the information?

- Quoting verbatim
- Editing the source
- Paraphrasing
- Summarising
- Sub-editorialising
- Taking information and ideas

Suggestions for an answer to this exercise may be found at the back of the book on page 89.

COMBINING DIFFERENT SOURCES

The biggest trap you can fall into when combining different sources is not to transform the language sufficiently. You have a new piece that you are going to write and it will have its own distinctive style to suit its audience and purpose. It is likely that the source texts you are using are not written in the same style as your new piece of writing. If you are dealing with several sources they are unlikely to share the same style. This is hardly surprising: they will all have been written for different audiences and purposes. A crucial step in preparing to write your own text is to assess and classify the language styles of your target and source texts. This will help you consider how to transform them.

Classifying Your Source Texts

As a first step to transforming texts successfully, it is helpful to be clear about the nature of the target text that you are going to write and the nature of the source texts that you have been given to use.

A first step will be to classify the text according to its key contextual determinants. Ask:

- Who was this text written by?
- Who is the audience for this text?
- What genre is this text?
- What are its purposes?
- What are its subject matter and content?
- In what context is it used?

It is then useful to think about the style of the text. Several linguists have used the idea of scales or dimensions as a way of classifying texts. In *Higher Level Differences between Speech and Writing* (Committee for Linguistics in Education, 1984), R.A. Hudson developed a series of dimensions to measure the mode of a text. He wanted to investigate the mode of a text in a more sophisticated way than just saying it was spoken or written. Table 6.2 draws on and extends his ideas.

When faced with a set of sources to adapt and use for a writing task you could fill in this chart for your target style (the way you need to write for the brief you have been given) and then for the styles of the source you have to use. If you were writing a fictionalised eyewitness account of the Irish Potato Famine to appear in a drama-documentary it might resemble the graph shown in Figure 6.2.

The differences between the target style and the styles of your sources will need to be reduced as you transform your materials and make use of them in your own piece. This classification process will also help you to harmonise the styles of different sources that you might be drawing on.

Table 6.2 Scales for assessing texts' style

	2	1	0	1	2	
Written						Spoken
Technical						Non-technical
Formal						Informal
Impersonal						Personal
Context free						Context dependent
Standard						Non-standard
Older						Contemporary
Complex vocabulary						Simple vocabulary
Non-interactive						Interactive
Complex grammar						Simple grammar

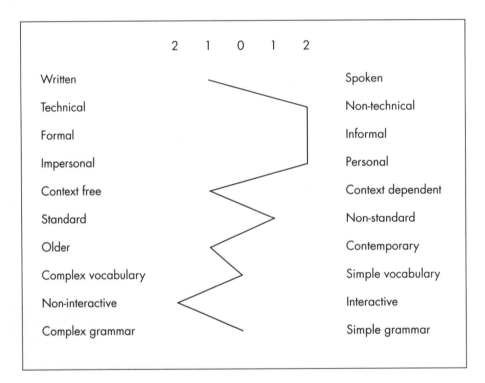

Figure 6.2 Assessing a text's style: a dramatic monologue

Sometimes you may be asked to comment on the ways in which you have adapted your sources to create your new text. Using this chart will give you a way to think about the kinds of textual transformation you have had to make. This will provide you with some helpful conceptualisations about the nature of writing.

Assessing the Style of a Text

You can carry out some interesting analyses of texts using a word processing package. These often have style checkers that will tell you about the length of sentences or the use of passives in a text. They often use readability calculations to tell you how complex a piece of writing is in terms of the demands it makes on the reader (Figure 6.3).

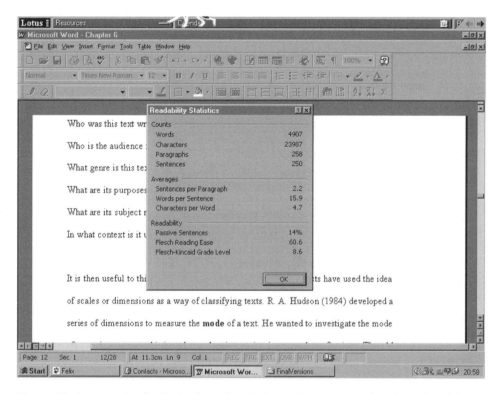

Figure 6.3 An example of style checker software that analyses sentence lengths and readability

Some software packages enable you to set the grammar and style checker at different levels. For example, it is possible in some software packages to check a piece of text as a casual, standard, formal or technical style.

In Figure 6.4, because the program is set to check a formal style, the contractions box is ticked. This is because contractions are not an acceptable feature of formal writing.

You can use the following exercises to help you think about different levels of style when you are practising editorial writing during your course.

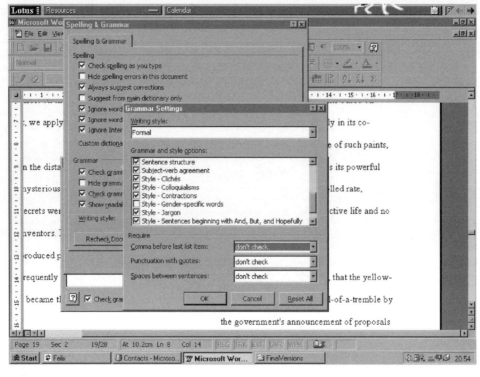

Figure 6.4 An example of style checker software that analyses more detailed features of style at different levels of formality

Exercise 2

Find out about the grammar and style checker on your word processor. What different styles will it check? What are the different features that it queries or checks at different style levels?

Scan a source text you have to use for a piece of transformational writing so that it is available as a word processor file. Check its style at the level of the text you have to transform it into. For example, use an informal text that you have to make more formal. What kinds of alterations do you need to make?

Scan an example of a type of text you have to write (e.g. a broadsheet feature article). Run it through the style checker. What paragraph and sentence lengths does it employ? Run your own feature article through the checker. Does your style match?

CASE STUDY 2 – A BROADSHEET FEATURE ARTICLE

Below is a feature article about the environmental effects of the paints used on the hulls of boats. We are going to use this article to explore what kinds of research and sources a writer uses and how they are then transformed into an article. We shall also practise some sub-editorial writing.

Exercise 3

- Identify the range of sources the writer must have used to produce the following article
- In what different ways has he used or re-presented his sources?
- How has the writer structured his argument and analysed his different sources?
- What effects has he created by the way he has introduced his quotations from his sources?

Exercise 4

- What kind of photograph would you want to select to go with the following article?
- Write the following sub-editorial elements for this article:

    - A headline
    - A fifty- to sixty-word sub-editorial introduction
    - Two pull quotes.

We boat owners have always had to paint our bottoms. Any craft kept afloat for long periods will rapidly acquire a colony of barnacles, limpets, weed, and other forms of marine life whose presence has a dramatic effect on the boat's performance. To prevent it, we apply antifouling paint.

In the distant past antifouling paints were mysterious concoctions whose poisonous secrets were jealously guarded by their inventors. More recently, commercially produced paints – based on copper, but frequently containing boosters such as arsenic – became the norm.

But these compounds had major disadvantages: they were difficult and hazardous to apply, their effective life was short, and the build-up of paint layers required periodic removal. The need to beach the boat or crane it ashore meant that several days' use could be lost each year.

These messy, time-consuming, and potentially hazardous chores have been much reduced by the advent of paints based on tributyl tin (TBT), particularly in its co-polymer form. The resin base of such paints, by slowly dissolving, releases its powerful antifouling agent at a controlled rate, resulting in an increased effective life and no build-up of paint.

It is not surprising, therefore, that the yellow-wellied fraternity were set all-of-a-

continued

tremble by the government's announcement of proposals to ban the sale of paints containing TBT. In conjunction with the paint manufacturers, yachtsmen's organisations – headed by the Royal Yachting Association – launched a heated campaign against the proposed ban.

At the centre of the case put by government scientists is *Crassostrea gigas*, the Pacific oyster, imported by growers to overcome problems with the native oyster. The new species is now itself declining, a situation attributed to the presence of TBT in the waters surrounding oyster beds. These waters, estuarial and for the most part shallow, frequently contain moorings for small craft, and hence the proposed ban relates only to boats of less than 12 metres (39 feet) in overall length.

Yachtsmen attacked the scientific basis of the argument, claiming that laboratory research was not directly applicable to the real situation. They pointed to the large tonnage of commercial shipping which might be using TBT. Many were the cries of 'Unfair.'

The campaigners, urged on by the paint manufacturers, became very excited; their arguments were not always entirely rational. Chauvinism often surfaced. The fact that the French have banned TBT was cited as a reason why we should not. And what right had nasty foreign oysters in our British waters, anyway?

This kind of irate bluster is best typified by a letter to the yachting press which referred to those in favour of the TBT ban as 'a rump of emotional wretches who seek some cause . . . typified by those that recently voted a large sum of ratepayers' money to an Irish lesbian group.'

But most of the coherent arguments centred on the oyster. The economic importance of oyster fishing was adversely compared with the large yachting industry. 'At the end of the day,' sniffed an editorial in *Yachting Monthly*, 'we are talking about a luxury delicacy against a type of paint developed to give us easier and safer sailing.' There are few oyster beds, some of them not close to yacht moorings. Was it therefore reasonable to ban the use of TBT on some 90,000 yachts 'at the behest of something called the Shellfish Association?' (Air Commodore John Chamier in *Yachts & Yachting*).

This kind of argument, not unnaturally, annoyed the oystermen. By degrees, the temperature of the debate climbed to the point where little rational analysis was possible. But there is now a moment of calm, while government considers the numerous submissions it has received in response to its proposals.

The argument became debased in part because the proposals – emanating from the Ministry of Agriculture, Fisheries, and Food – were badly presented. The emphasis on oysters permits many arguments that would have been excluded by a wider ecological case. The proposals were also draconian, sudden, and to a degree traitorous – yachtsmen saw themselves sold down the river by their own government. The paint manufacturers have encouraged an unthinking response for cogent commercial reasons: antifouling paints represent a disproportionate percentage of their profits. Major manufacturers such as International Paints and Blakes sell TBT antifouling at a minimum of £13 per litre. As even a small yacht requires some five litres each year, it is an attractive market. Even the least affluent yottie can only wince and pay up.

As a result, the broad issue of antifouling paints and their effect on the environment has been obscured. Conservationists who have attempted to widen the argument have been ignored. One such defender of the marine environment is Maldwin Drummond, 40 years a yachtsman, and also a Countryside Commissioner. His view, frequently and powerfully stated to all concerned, is that oysters are best seen as a sensitive indicator of the harm that TBT can do. Although the oyster industry is important in itself, the overriding concern must be for the whole marine environment.

There is in fact a large body of scientific work which analyses the effects of TBT on a wide range of marine species, including clams, crabs, shrimps, Dover sole, algae, and plankton. For example, a paper was presented to the Estuarine and Coastal Pollution Conference in Plymouth last week by A. R. Beaumont and P. B. Newman of the Marine Science Laboratory, University College of North Wales. They show that tiny amounts of TBT – between 0.2 and 0.5 parts per billion – are harmful to marine microalgae, the basis of the food chain. At risk, therefore, is not just the oyster but the complete shallow water ecology.

But the views of conservationists and of respectable scientific establishments continue to be rejected by bodies such as the Royal Yachting Association. This is the more remarkable in that all yachtsmen are presented with obvious evidence of the overcrowding of our estuaries and rivers. In the Solent area, these are the typical figures for numbers of yachts moored afloat: river Hamble, 3,100; Cowes, 1,223; Lymington, 1,800; Portsmouth, 2,500; Chichester, 4,950; Poole, 5,711. The total number of yachts moored between Chichester and Poole is 23,825. From this figure we can calculate that around a third of a million square metres of (mostly) TBT antifouling paint is exposed in estuarial waters.

TBT is, of course, a highly toxic material deliberately introduced into the water to kill marine life. Therefore it is certain to be harmful to the general marine environment – as indeed is any toxic antifouling compound. Whatever action the government finally decides to take, we should find time for rational debate and, particularly, calm the panic reaction of yachtsmen. Alternatives to TBT do exist. An embargo will not stop us painting our bottoms, but it will reduce the risk to our precious coastal waters.

© Martin Corrick published in the *Guardian*, 27 July 1985

Suggestions for Answer to Exercise 3

The writer seems to have used the following sources:

- The case put by government scientists – summarised
- A letter to the yachting press – edited quotation
- An editorial in the magazine *Yachting Monthly* – quoted
- Air Commodore John Chamier in the magazine *Yachts & Yachting* – paraphrased and quoted
- Proposals from the Ministry of Agriculture, Fisheries, and Food – summarised and interpreted
- The price lists of paint manufacturers – example given

- Maldwin Drummond, forty years a yachtsman, and also a Countryside Commissioner – summarised and reported
- A paper presented to the Estuarine and Coastal Pollution Conference in Plymouth the previous week by A. R. Beaumont and P. B. Newman of the Marine Science Laboratory, University College of North Wales – summarised

The writer has used phrases such as 'In the distant past' to indicate his survey of what used to happen before TBTs. As the article progresses, he tries to move between the arguments for and against the use of TBTs, creating a sense of a dramatic argument between opposing sides. He frequently uses the word 'argument' to identify the various views and positions of the different sides in the debate. On two occasions he uses the conjunction 'But' to indicate a contrasting argument. The expression 'As a result' is used to show the consequences of the behaviour of the paint manufacturers and he uses words such as 'therefore' to show the way he is trying to establish a reasoned conclusion. At the end of the article the phrase 'of course' seeks agreement from the reader as a final point of view is established. Such phrases can be used very helpfully to link ideas and sources together and signal the structure of a new text.

One of the quotations used is labelled as 'irate bluster', suggesting it is emotional and insubstantial as a point of view. Another quotation is introduced using the verb 'sniffed' which judges the view as self-important.

Suggestions for Answer to Exercise 4

The original photograph that accompanied this article showed lots of closely packed yachts. The caption was 'The river Hamble: 3,100 yachts in 2½ miles of narrow waterway'. This tried to stress the scale of the problem.

The original headline for this article was the rather dramatic 'Killer Yachts'. The sub-editorial introduction ran as follows:

> The Government is for once on the side of the angels in proposing to ban a highly toxic paint which is destroying marine life in our estuaries. But the proposal has upset not only the paint manufacturers but their customers, the yellow wellied fraternity. Martin Corrick, himself a yachtsman, argues that as the paint is deliberately concocted to kill barnacles and limpet and weed, it is inevitably harmful to the environment.

PUTTING IT ALL TOGETHER

When you write your new text, using sources, you will need to go through a process of making some major decisions followed by some very small and precise decisions about your new writing style.

1. Assess what it is you have to do. Who is your audience and what are your purposes? What genre or kind of text have you got to write? What sort of style is going to be necessary for your new text?
2. Assess your sources. What content do they contain that you could use for your new text? What is their language like? How will you need to adapt it and re-present the material?
3. Get an angle on your materials. What is the big issue or idea you want to communicate? How will you structure your text?
4. Plan your communicative strategies. Make your macro decisions (see below).
5. Write your text. Make your micro decisions (see below).
6. Edit and revise your text.

Macro Decisions

You need to think about the broad presentational features of the text you are going to produce. You should consider the ways you are going to transform the nature of your sources. For example, you could use diaries, letters, dialogues, characters, exposition, narratives and stories, word boxes, timelines, boxed information, bullets, summaries, subsections, headings, pictures, tables, graphs.

Micro Decisions

As you adapt your texts and write your own piece you will need to ensure that you are transforming the language of your sources sufficiently.

Discourse level

- Is your text made up of the necessary elements (e.g. main text, text boxes, lists, photographs)?
- Are your paragraphs the right length?
- Have you used the necessary sub-editorial elements?
- Does your text address your audience appropriately?
- Is your text cohesive? Have you given the reader signals about the way the text is linked? Is the text consistent and coherent?

Sentence level

- Are you using the appropriate range of sentence functions? For example, have you added in or removed questions or commands?
- Are your sentences of the right type? Have you transformed the style of the sources? Does your use of minor, simple, compound, complex or **compound-complex sentences** match the target style?
- How long are your sentences? Is there the right number of clauses or words to match your target style?

Grammatical level

- Are you using the appropriate tenses?
- Are you using the progressive aspect?
- Are you using active or passive verbs?
- Are **modal auxiliary verbs** helpful?

Word level

- How descriptive is your language? Are you using the appropriate number of adjectives and adverbs?
- Is your word choice designed to be dramatic? persuasive? neutral and objective?
- How formal is your language?
- Is your vocabulary Anglo-Saxon or Latinate?
- How technical is your vocabulary?
- Do you need to gloss or explain vocabulary?
- Have you used figurative language?

SUMMARY

In this chapter we have looked at:

- Different ways of using sources
- How to combine sources
- How to adopt an appropriate style for your own new texts

This should help you:

- Carry out editorial or recasting writing tasks where you have to use and re-present source materials
- Write effective coursework pieces where you carry out research to provide you with the content of your piece
- Demonstrate the skills of reading and writing required for the Level 3 Key Skills qualification in Communication

---

SUGGESTIONS FOR ANSWER

CHAPTER 2, EXERCISE 1

Below you will find a transformed version of the Huon pine text. This is not a 'correct' answer. There are many other ways you could transform this text.

> ### History
>
> People have valued the wood of the Huon pine highly ever since the early days when Europeans first came to Tasmania. They set up a convict settlement* on Sarah Island, Macquarie Harbour in 1821. This was done so that they could harvest Huon pine from the Gordon River.
>
> For decades 'piners'* cut down trees along the west coast rivers. Working conditions were very hard. They cut down trees along the river banks and on the nearby slopes.
>
> The Huon pine is one of the few trees in Tasmania which floats when it has just been cut down. The 'piners' carried the trees by hand to the river edges. When the rivers flooded, the waters carried the logs downstream. Men in boats freed jammed logs and kept them moving on their way. The logs finally came to a barrier built across the river to stop them. The 'piners' then took the logs to the mills.*

* This text would also be accompanied by a word box in which terms such as 'piners', 'mills' and 'convict settlements' would be explained. It could also be accompanied by a map of Tasmania showing where the tree cutting took place.

Commentary: Changes to Vocabulary

A frequent type of change is to replace words with basic core synonyms. This makes the vocabulary simpler. In the first sentence the word 'timber' has been altered to the more basic 'wood'. 'Gruelling' has been replaced by 'hard'. More general terms are used instead of more precise synonyms. Boat is used instead of 'punt'.

At times it has been necessary to explain what a word refers to and means. The word 'colony' has been defined by a clause explaining the action that creates a colony. A gloss has been used to explain the terms 'convict settlement', 'mills' and 'piners'. To transform these within the text itself would have been quite cumbersome.

The number of different vocabulary items has been reduced. There is deliberate repetition in the use of 'cut down trees', 'logs' and 'piners'. This enables the reader to focus on the ideas rather than dealing with variation in style. The **cohesive ties** in the text are made more obvious through this use of **lexical repetition**. Pronoun usage has also been avoided to keep the ideas as clear as possible. The reader does not have to make links back to previous sentences to decode what is being said. Extra cohesive ties are created when the difficult word 'native' is transformed in the phrase 'in Tasmania'.

Words with rather unusual usages have also been transformed. The verb 'worked' has a rather obscure meaning here, especially because of its object, the river. It has been replaced with 'cut down trees' which describes the actions in a more concrete way. The meaning of green is more than just a colour reference and this has been more fully explained.

Some vocabulary has been deleted. The technical term 'alluvial' has been removed. As an adjective it does not significantly add information about where the trees were taken from.

Commentary: Changes to Grammar

Throughout the transformation sentence lengths are shortened. Most sentences have one or two clauses. The number of ideas per sentence is kept low.

In the original the first paragraph was complex and abstract in style. This is because it employs passives such as 'has been . . . prized' and verbs without subjects such as 'establishing' and 'harvesting'. These processes have been made more concrete by the addition of some human subjects: 'People' and 'they'.

CHAPTER 3, EXERCISE 2

There is no right answer to this activity. You may have put sentence breaks in different places from those in the text on page 20. It depends on how you interpret the way the spoken ideas fit together. Here is one possible example.

Well, I suppose it looked something like a baked bean tin on the front that had a lot of holes in it. The rest was rubber that went right over the whole of your face, underneath your chin, round towards your ears and over your head. You couldn't breathe particularly easily. It was like when you went to the dentist or had gas at the dentist. You fought against it for a bit but you got used to the idea and that's why, of course, we had lessons with them to get used to the idea. If you were sensible they didn't fog up and you could cope.

CHAPTER 3, EXERCISE 3

The following is a version of the audiotape with the non-fluency features and non-verbal aspects of speech edited out.

so what have I been doing well yesterday was Monday and I was in the office all day and I discovered that I've got a new Side by Side class yes that's exactly what I need so I'm doing nine hours of Side by Side in one week do you know Sonia's never taught Side by Side and she's been here for over a year and a half but still we can't all have the pleasure of knowing the text backwards can we I'm back to page twenty-seven now which I can tell without thinking about it is where's Patti Williams what's she doing and to be honest Patti Williams is really irritating because she's forever cleaning her bicycle in the parking lot which is like one of those completely meaningless sentences anyway yeah Sunday was cool probably told you so yeah I must've done I met my new extra-curricular Japanese teacher who's called Tomoko To mo ko which I don't really like as a Japanese name it's too masculine Tom Tomoko but she's really nice as I say she's 23 she's in the same situation as me and I probably told you we sat for two hours and discussed exactly what actions to do to Twinkle Twinkle Little Star it was quite cool I've just been faffing around and I did my usual stuff on a Sunday night I get my cleaning stuff out and I do all my washing up and all my drying up and stuff like that and I clean my stove and do my fridge and I do my washing and some ironing and stuff like that and actually yesterday I decided to buy a pinny which was probably one of the saddest things I've ever bought but they do have some nice ones over here it's kind of catching most Japanese housewifey women wear these kind of overall jobs I think you call it a tabard

A variety of features have been removed in this edited version of Text C:

Non-fluency Features

Fillers	but erm (1.0) she's really nice
Pauses	and I (.) probably told you
Hesitations/intakes of breath	.h yesterday was Monday
False starts	which I st. which I don't really like as a Japanese name it's too f. masculine
Repetition	I'm I'm back to page um twenty-seven now

Pronunciation Features

Non-verbal vocalisations	still huh we can't all have the pleasure (1.0) of knowing the text backwards
Pauses for effect	Tomoko (.) To (.) mo (.) ko (.)
Omission of /d/	an' I clean my stove an' do my fridge
Elongations of words	ye::s that's exactly what I need

CHAPTER 3, EXERCISE 4

The version of the audiotape below has had sentence punctuation inserted. You may have done this slightly differently. The daughter did not speak into her tape with sentences in mind – we are altering and making an interpretation of what she said and meant when we add in the punctuation.

Although sentence punctuation has been added there are differences between the grammar of this version and what are seen as the typical grammatical features of writing. Four segments have been emboldened because they raise issues about the nature of spoken and written grammar. They are discussed further after the rewritten version of the tape.

So what have I been doing? Well, yesterday was Monday and I was in the office all day, and I discovered that I've got a new 'Side by Side' class. Yes, that's exactly what I need! So I'm doing nine hours of 'Side by Side' in one week. Do you know Sonia's never taught 'Side by Side', and she's been here for over a year and a half, but still we can't all have the pleasure of knowing the text backwards, can we? **I'm back to page twenty-seven now which I can tell without thinking about it is, 'Where's Patti Williams? What's she doing?' and to be honest Patti Williams is really irritating because she's forever cleaning her bicycle in the parking lot, which is, like, one of those completely meaningless sentences.**[1]

Anyway, yeah, Sunday was cool. **Probably told you so.**[2] Yeah, I must've done. I met my new extra-curricular Japanese teacher who's called Tomoko,

To-mo-ko, which I don't really like as a Japanese name. It's too masculine: Tom Tomoko, but she's really nice, as I say. **She's 23. She's in the same situation as me and I probably told you we sat for two hours and discussed exactly what actions to do to Twinkle Twinkle Little Star.**[3] It was quite cool.

I've just been faffing around and I did my usual stuff on a Sunday night. **I get my cleaning stuff out and I do all my washing up and all my drying up and stuff like that, and I clean my stove and do my fridge and I do my washing and some ironing and stuff like that and actually yesterday I decided to buy a pinny, which was probably one of the saddest things I've ever bought, but they do have some nice ones over here.**[4] It's kind of catching. Most Japanese housewifey women wear these kind of overall jobs. I think you call it a tabard.

The grammar of spoken language tends to be different from writing. Clauses are often left loosely side by side or are joined by **co-ordinating conjunctions**. **Subordination** is much more common in writing. This is a big generalisation, however, and both styles can be found. None the less, typical speech tends to have a less complex grammatical structure than typical writing.

The emboldened segment 1 might be better rewritten further and separated into two sentences. At the moment its structure is typically spoken. Even though it contains subordinate clauses, it is like speech because of the way it piles up clauses where writing might tend to create more sentence boundaries.

I'm back to page twenty-seven now which I can tell without thinking about it is 'Where's Patti Williams? What's she doing?' To be honest Patti Williams is really irritating because she's forever cleaning her bicycle in the parking lot which is, like, one of those completely meaningless sentences.

Segment 2 is an instance of ellipsis. In written language we might transform this by supplying the subject 'I'. By doing so, however, we might make the letter more formal than the daughter might want in the circumstances.

Segment 3 is only one way of rewriting this section. The clauses 'she's 23' and 'she's in the same situation as me' are typical of speech in the way they are placed loosely side by side. In writing we might join them together. The element 'and I probably told you' might be treated differently in writing. Instead of using co-ordination, either a sentence boundary or a subordinating conjunction could be inserted. In written text we could remove a further co-ordinating conjunction from this section to make it more like written language.

> She's 23 and in the same situation as me so, I probably told you, we sat for two hours discussing exactly what actions to do to Twinkle Twinkle Little Star.[3]

Segment 4 has a lot of co-ordinating conjunctions in it which seem to be typical of speech grammar. However, we might want to leave some of them in a written transformation because they are actually there for a rhetorical effect. The daughter is seeking to show the extent of the boring routine her life has become. We might make a change by deleting the word 'and' before 'actually'. Here she moves on to a different topic which merits a new sentence in written language. On the other hand you might feel that buying the pinny is intended as the comic climax of her terrible decline into adult domesticity and retain it. This is the kind of stylistic choice you could discuss in a commentary on this sort of task.

> I get my cleaning stuff out and I do all my washing up and all my drying up and stuff like that and I clean my stove and do my fridge and I do my washing and some ironing and stuff like that. Actually yesterday I decided to buy a pinny which was probably one of the saddest things I've ever bought but they do have some nice ones over here.[4]

CHAPTER 3, EXERCISE 8

Here is a possible transformation of the Solomon Northup text:

> Only rest I ever gits from never-ending work is during them Christmas holidays. Old Master Epps 'llowed us three days – other masters tho', they was more generous, they 'llowed maybe four, five even six days! Only time I ever gits to look forward to anything at all. I's glad when night comes and it ain't just 'cos I gits a few hours of sleep, no sir, it's 'cos I's one mo' day closer to Christmas. Young 'uns, old 'uns – we all rejoices when it comes. Even Uncle Abram he stops his praising Andrew Jackson and that Patsy, she forgit all her woes, mid all the happiness and hilarity. We feasts and we frolics, we sings and we dances. These be the only days when we sees a little freedom and we sure makes the most of it.

Sample Commentary

In my creation of the character's voice I have used features that reflect the spoken channel of speech and try to convey the actual sounds of his language. Some words are spelt to suggest his accent: 'gits', 'mo''.

I have also tried to use language that would simulate the face-to-face and spontaneous situation of speaking. I have used first-person pronouns such as 'I' to reflect the speaking situation and the recounting of memories and experiences. My transformation makes use of ellipsis to suggest the grammar of speech: I have left out 'the' at the very start of the piece. I have used the present tense to simulate typical oral narrative style and to create a sense of immediacy.

I have tried to make the character sound American. I have used some non-standard verb forms such as 'I's' rather than 'I'm', and American idioms such as the use of 'sure'. I have also used non-standard demonstratives such as 'them' for 'those'.

CHAPTER 4, EXERCISE 9

Below are some possible ways of changing the sentence structures of the original Elihu Burritt article to make it appropriate for use in a radio documentary.

> 4. Seeing a cabin standing somewhat by itself in a hollow, and surrounded by a moat of green filth, we entered it with some difficulty. *Inside we* found a single child about three years old lying on a kind of shelf. *Its* little face rested upon the edge of the board and looked steadfastly out of the door as if for its mother.

The original sentence has been turned into three by removing a co-ordinating conjunction and inserting a subject. Two **non-finite clauses** have been made **finite** and converted into a separate sentence.

> 5. *I doubt* whether the poor thing had a mother or father left to her. *I doubt even more* whether those eyes would have relaxed their vacant gaze if both of them had entered at once with anything that could tempt the palate in their hands.

Again the original sentence has been changed into two. The impersonal expression 'It is doubtful' has been turned into a more personal expression. It has been repeated to retain the parallel structure Burritt creates.

> 6. *I have never seen* such bright, blue, clear eyes looking so steadfastly at nothing.

In this sentence the change has created a more conventional word order by placing the subject at the front. However, we should consider other issues when transforming this text as well. Are there occasions when our transformation might make the text less effective? Here Burritt's original stresses the word 'never' by putting it at the front of the clause. We may also want to retain some features that make the text sound older in style to evoke the historical period.

CHAPTER 5, EXERCISE 3

Transforming this extract from Jane Austen's novel presents a number of challenges. Although it has two characters and plenty of direct speech, unlike the original version of *Fever Pitch* that we looked at, it still needs quite a lot of transformation to make it work as a screenplay.

Some of the main writing issues to be tackled are:

- Conveying the thoughts of the characters that Austen reveals through her narrative
- Cutting the very long speeches and creating a sense of dramatic cut-and-thrust dialogue
- Maintaining cohesion after making cuts
- Transforming Austen's long sentences to utterances that can be understood easily by a listener
- Retaining a sense of period language

As one example of the various ways the sequence could be transformed, here is an extract from the screenplay for Ang Lee's film of the novel. The screenplay was written by Emma Thompson.

Text C: *Sense and Sensibility* – Screenplay

ELINOR: But your behaviour to him in all other respects is perfectly cordial so I must assume that you like him in spite of his deficiencies.

MARIANNE [*trying hard*]: I think him everything that is amiable and worthy.

ELINOR: Praise indeed!

MARIANNE: But he shall have my unanswering devotion when you tell me he is to be my brother.

[ELINOR *is greatly taken aback and does not know how to reply. Suddenly* MARIANNE *hugs her passionately.*]

MARIANNE: How shall I do without you?

ELINOR: Do without me?

[MARIANNE *pulls away, her eyes full of tears.*]

MARIANNE: I am sure you will be very happy. But you must promise not to live *too* far away.

ELINOR: Marianne, there is no question of – that is, there is no understanding between. . . .

[ELINOR *trails off.* MARIANNE *looks at her keenly.*]

MARIANNE: Do you love him?

[*The bold clarity of this question discomforts* ELINOR.]

ELINOR: I do not attempt to deny that I think very highly of him – that I greatly esteem – that I *like* him.

MARIANNE: Esteem him! Like him! Use those insipid words again and I shall leave the room this instant!

[*This makes* ELINOR *laugh in spite of her discomfort.*]

ELINOR: Very well. Forgive me. Believe my feelings to be stronger than I have declared – but further than that you must not believe.

[MARIANNE *is flummoxed but she rallies swiftly and picks up her book again.*]

MARIANNE: 'Is love a fancy or a feeling?' Or a Ferrars?

ELINOR: Go to bed!

[ELINOR *blushes in good earnest.* MARIANNE *goes to the door.*]

MARIANNE [*imitating Elinor*]: I do not attempt to deny that I think highly of him — greatly esteem him! *Like* him!

[*And she is gone, leaving* ELINOR *both agitated and amused.*]

Emma Thompson, *Sense and Sensibility – The Screenplay*, 1995

Layout and Presentation

This screenplay is presented in a similar layout to Hornby's. This is an extract from a longer scene but the numbering and time and place descriptions are similar when it begins. Italicised sections are used again to describe actions and emotions. They are in the present tense, and make use of adjectives and adverbs.

Dialogue

Unlike Hornby's original text, Austen's novel presents quite a lot of dialogue that could be used. Thompson has used some sequences in a verbatim manner, but has cut a lot of the dialogue from the original. She does not use Elinor's discussion of her relationship with Ferrars and moves straight to asking Marianne's opinion. Long set-piece speeches are thus avoided for more interactive dialogue. A high proportion of the sentences are exclamations, questions and commands which create the sense of pacy dialogue. Generally Thompson's sentences are much shorter and she has simplified grammatical constructions.

Dramatising Thoughts

At the beginning, the screenplay has to dramatise Elinor's perceptions about Marianne's and her mother's tendency to jump to conclusions and their belief that she is as good as married to Ferrars already. In the novel this is revealed by the narrator's explanation. In the screenplay it is realised by Marianne getting upset about the prospect of Elinor living elsewhere: 'How shall I do without you?' Thompson allows this sequence to extend over four utterances to create a sense of conflict between the sisters and to convey how Marianne has convinced herself of a wedding that is far from guaranteed.

Words such as the adjective 'insipid' have been added to clarify the views of a character when the narrative comment about Marianne's indignation is not present.

Creating Period Voices

Thompson has also used italicisation to create a greater sense of tone of voice. She does not have verbs of saying such as 'burst forth' to help her indicate how characters speak. She is careful to retain vocabulary such as 'declared' and 'understanding' to convey the period.

Maintaining Cohesion

Thompson has had to be careful to maintain cohesion after her editing of Elinor's speeches. Where Austen has 'Believe them', Thompson writes 'Believe my feelings'. The pronoun needs changing because there is no previous reference to feelings now that part of Austen's dialogue has been cut.

CHAPTER 6, EXERCISE 1

Table 6.3 Ways of using sources in different types of writing

	Display boards	Drama-documentary	Children's history book
Quoting verbatim	✔		
Editing the source	✔		
Paraphrasing	✔		✔
Summarising	✔		✔
Sub-editorialising	✔		✔
Taking information	✔	✔	✔

For the display boards you might choose to quote directly, possibly with some editing, from works of historians that you have read in your sources. Here you could use your sources quite directly.

For the drama-documentary you might want to use a narrator, some dialogue and possibly the monologue of a character you have created. You would need to move a long way from the language of your sources.

You might present the diary of a character as part of the children's book. On the other hand you might provide some straightforward exposition on the topic where you summarise or paraphrase parts of your sources.

GLOSSARY

Active verb   In the active voice, the subject in a clause is the agent who carries out an action: *He dropped the book*. In the passive (see page 94) the affected (the person or object an action is performed on) becomes the subject. *The book was dropped by the man*

Adjectives   A word class with a descriptive function

Adverbial   A clause element. It can consist of one word or several. Adverbials can convey information about when an action took place, where and why it occurred

Adverbs   A word class that describes verbs and adjectives in terms of manner, time, place, degree

Allusion   A reference to something beyond the text, presupposing the audience's knowledge

Articles   Examples of determiners. 'The' is called the **definite article**. It refers to a specific thing: *the particular cat I am talking about*. 'A' or 'an' are called the indefinite article. They refer to any example of something: *I am talking about a cat* wihout specifying a particular one

Auxiliary verbs   The primary auxiliary verbs are to have and to be. These are used with main verbs that carry the main lexical meaning. The auxiliary verbs are used to convey information about time and duration: *He is finishing now. They have already finished*

Clause   A group of words that cluster around a verb, sometimes containing a subject, object, complement and adverbials

Cohesion   The way texts hold together. May be demonstrated lexically by words from similar fields linking together. May also occur grammatically through the reference links between pronouns and the nouns they have replaced

Colloquial   Used to describe the level of formality of language. It refers to ordinary, everyday usage that is not formal

Comment clause   A clause inserted into a sentence to pass comment on what is being said: 'That is very unlikely, *I have to say*'

Complex sentence   A sentence of two or more clauses linked by subordinating conjunctions

Compound-complex sentence   A sentence of three or more clauses with some linked by co-ordinating conjunctions and others linked by subordinating conjunctions

Compound sentence   A sentence of two or more clauses linked by co-ordinating conjunctions

Connotation   The associations that a word conveys in addition to its literal meaning. The word 'apple' might connote health

Co-ordinating conjunction   A joining word that links ideas of relative equality: *and, or, but*

Definite article   A determiner that precedes a noun, identifying a specific reference: '*the* cup' (as opposed to the indefinite article '*a* cup')

Deixis   The pointing functions of words such as *this/that here/now* which are often context dependent for their meaning in speech

Demonstratives   Words that demonstrate particular references: *this/that these/those*, may act as an adjective and precede a noun, *Take this cup*, or as a pronoun replacing the noun, *Take this*

Denotation   The literal meaning of a word. 'Apple', for example, refers to a particular kind of fruit

Determiners   Words which precede a noun and determine its reference: *a/the/my/that car*

Dialect   A distinctive variety of language, often revealing the regional, social and ethnic origins of a speaker

Discourse markers   Words such as *well, so, anyway* that signal links or boundaries between parts of a text

Ellipsis   The omission of elements from within a clause or phrase: *Shan't* for *(I) shan't (tell you)*

False starts   A feature of speech where a speaker begins to say something but does not complete what they are saying

Fillers   Small utterances such as *um* and *er* used to prevent silence when talking

Finite clause   A clause with a verb which is defined in terms of person (who did the action) and tense (when it happened)

Grammatical blends   A feature of speech where a speaker begins with one structure but completes with another: '*the rest was rubber that went (.) right over covered the whole of your face*'

Iambic pentameter   A description of patterns or rhythm in poetry. A pentameter is made up of five units called feet. Each foot is made up of a pattern of stressed and unstressed syllables. An iambic foot is made up of an unstressed syllable followed by a stressed syllable.

Ideology   The characteristic ways of thinking, beliefs and values that belong to an individual or a group

Idiolectal   Adjective derived from the noun 'idiolect'. An idiolect is an individual's distinctive way of using language

Imperative   A form of the verb which conveys a command or acts as a directive

Indefinite pronoun   A pronoun without reference to a particular person, e.g. *anyone, someone*

Inflection   A word ending that is added to indicate tense, aspect, person or plurality, e.g. *walk-ed, go-ing, house-s, he hope-s*

Lexical repetition   A form of cohesion. Sentences can hang together as part of a text by repeating words which reveal the sentences' interconnectedness

Minor sentence   A sentence without a finite verb but with a capital letter and full stop

Modal auxiliary verb   A special group of auxiliary verbs conveying meanings about obligation, permission, ability and likelihood, e.g. *can, may, might, should*, etc.

Mode   A text's mode refers to the medium by which the language is transmitted, e.g. speech, writing or e-language

Multi-word verb   A verb made up of several words, often a verb with an adverb or a preposition, e.g. '*look up* a reference'

Non-finite clause A clause with a non-finite verb, i.e. a participle or an infinitive

Non-fluency features These are found in some forms of speech and reflect the fact that they are produced spontaneously, without preparation and without the ability to be revised. Pauses, fillers, hesitations, false starts, unintended repetitions and grammatical blends are types of non-fluency

Object A clause element identifying who or what is affected by the verb and action

Passive verb In the active voice, the subject in a clause is the agent who carries out an action: *He dropped the book*. In the passive the affected (the person or object an action is performed on) becomes the subject: *The book was dropped by the man*. This transformation is created by the use of the auxiliary verb 'to be' and the past participle. The agent is referred to in an agentive phrase *by-*. This may be omitted: *The book was dropped*

Past participle A non-finite form of the verb usually created by adding -ed to the base. Used to form the perfect tense

Pauses Momentary silences during speech

Perfect An aspect of the verb formed by the auxiliary verb 'to have' and the main verb in its past participle form. Conveys the idea of an action being completed but of current relevance: *I have bought a house* in contrast to *I bought a house*

Person Used to describe pronouns in terms of whom they refer to: first person (*I/we*), second person (*you/you*) or third person (*he/she/it/they*). Also used to identify finite verbs in terms of who carried out the action

Plurality Refers to the way a noun such as *house* can be changed to mean more than one, e.g. *houses*

Possessive adjective A determiner with a pronominal function as well. Precedes a noun to determine to whom the noun belongs, e.g. *my coat, her cat*, etc.

Prepositional phrase A group of words beginning with a preposition, e.g. '*in* the middle of nowhere', '*over* the hill', etc.

Progressive An aspect of the verb formed by using the auxiliary verb *to be* and the present participle of the verb (the -ing form): *they are winning*. Conveys an ongoing action and a sense of duration

Pronouns A word class that is used to replace nouns. Pronouns may be singular or plural. They can be first person (*I/we*), second person (*you/you*) or third person (*he/she/it/they*). Pronouns change their form depending on their function in a particular sentence

Proper nouns   These are nouns that are the name of someone or something. They are marked with capital letters

Semantic field   A group of words that come from the same area of meaning

Sentence   A group of words in writing demarcated by an initial capital letter and a final full stop

Simple sentence   A sentence made up of only one clause

Standard English   A non-regional dialect of English. It is the variety of English used in newspapers and education. It refers to choices of grammar and vocabulary. It is not an accent

Starter   A word or phrase such as *well* or *right then* used at the beginning of an utterance to signal that the speaker is about to begin and to gain attention

Subject   A clause element identifying to whom the action or verb is ascribed

Subordinating conjunction   A linking word which ties in a secondary idea to a main idea, e.g. *while, because*. Introduces a subordinate clause

Suffix   An element that may be added at the end of a word, e.g. *-ed, -ly, etc.*

Syllable   A block of pronunciation within a word. It usually contains a vowel with consonants before or after it

Synonyms   Words with virtually the same meaning

Tense   The feature of finite verbs which indicates time, e.g. *past* or *present*

Verbs   A word class. Verbs describe actions, processes and states